STEELHEAD UNIVERSITY

YOUR GUIDE
TO SALMON & STEELHEAD SUCCESS

by Terry J. Wiest

Frank Amato Publications
Portland, OR

STEELHEAD UNIVERSITY

YOUR GUIDE TO SALMON & STEELHEAD SUCCESS

by Terry J. Wiest

Frank Amato
Publications
Portland, OR

DEDICATION

To the best fishing partner a guy could ever have:
My Dad, Oscar Wiest (1932 – 2001)

ACKNOWLEDGEMENTS

Thank you to the following individuals, without their contributions and support this book would not have been written:

First and foremost I must thank my loving wife of 25 years, Theresa, for her ongoing support and encouragement that keeps my passion for fishing alive.

I would also like to thank my good friend Tom Nelson who brought me onboard to Salmon and Steelhead University in 2006. Who would have known then how successful this venture would become. A true mentor and friend, Tom has taught me so much, both directly and indirectly.

To the many fishing partners over the years with whom I've shared lifelong memories and continue to learn from, with special thanks to: Phil Stephens, Mike Zavadlov, Todd Girtz, Brad Pott, Buzz Ramsey, Mike Perusse, Tom Pollack and Terry Rudnick.

I need to thank my old friend Dusty Routh (1960 – 2007) for giving me my first writing opportunity. And to Andy Walgamott for carrying on what Dusty had started and whom continues to support my writing efforts.

To Wayne Heinz and Steve Turner who set me in the right direction and helped me throughout this long process.

To my publisher, Frank Amato Publications, for entrusting me with this project that has been a longtime dream.

And to new friends I continue to meet on the water, I hope you enjoy this book.

©2012 Terry J. Wiest

All inquiries should be addressed to:
Frank Amato Publications, Inc.
P.O. Box 82112 • Portland, Oregon 97282
www.amatobooks.com • (503) 653-8108

All photos by Terry Wiest unless otherwise noted
Frontispiece photo by Jimmy Davis
Title page photo by Terry Wiest
Cover photo by Gil McKean

SB ISBN-13: 978-1-57188-501-2   SB UPC: 0-81127-00347-1

Printed in China

1 3 5 7 9 10 8 6 4 2

CONTENTS

INTRODUCTION

It's not quite 6:00 a.m. yet and my buddy and I have already hiked a mile and a half to our favorite fishing spot. The temperature is just below freezing but I've built up a sweat from the hike in. We take a minute to put our gear down and assess how we will attack the hole. The only light is from the moon and stars bouncing off the river. Water height is perfect and we can feel a good day about to unfold.

We both wade slowly so as not to disturb any fish that might be near. The only sounds are the trickle of the water coming downstream, and my heart as it pounds with excitement. We begin to cast slightly upstream. As it is still too dark to see our presentation hit the water, we rely on past experience and the sound of the lead hitting the water. As the line tightens up I can feel the lead hitting bottom, in fact dragging it. Realizing I have too much lead on, I quickly reel up, snip a small piece off and recast. Now as the line tightens I feel a slight "tick" every few seconds...now this is nice.

The sun has not yet broken over the horizon but we can start to make out the other side of the river and the defined holes. Now I can see where my lead is hitting, but I'm still not able to track my line. My rod is telegraphing everything on the other end as I'm relying on the feel and my instinct to let me know should a steelhead decide to mouth my presentation. Tick, tick, tick...

"There's one," I say in an excited but light voice.

"You got him?"

"Yep, fish on."

"Cool."

Not much talking between us but inside I'm one happy puppy.

My fishing partner retreats and puts his rod on the bank. I'm not able to see the fish but definitely know he doesn't want to come to shore. As I get him closer to me I begin to retreat myself but he doesn't want any part of me and high-tails it back to the safety of the hole. What an awesome sound as it strips line effortlessly from my reel.

The first hint of daylight arises and now as the fish comes near again we see him, a nice 8- to 10-pound buck and chrome bright as the silver sides reflect what light there is.

Again he strips line, this time breaking the surface as a loud splash now interrupts the peace of the flowing river.

He's getting tired now and I maneuver him once again near shore. This time there's not much fight left and my partner quickly tails him. The hook is removed from his upper jaw near the snout and my buddy asks if I want a picture.

"Nope, he's ready to go."

Making sure he's ready on his own, he's released to the river again and sends a splash of water onto my buddy's face.

We knuckle bump and we're back at it again.

Welcome to the world of salmon and steelhead fishing.

It is my desire that everyone that reads *Steelhead University: Your Guide to Salmon & Steelhead Success* is able to experience moments like this throughout their lifetime. These are moments I cherish and will never forget.

Most of us in the Pacific Northwest take for granted that we have salmon and steelhead in our waters. The Great Lakes, California, Canada and Alaska are also fortunate to have these amazing creatures. Those that live elsewhere can only dream of catching such beautiful fish. Having them around us is one thing, actually fishing for and catching them is a whole different experience. For many of us it's relaxation. For some it is a weekend activity. For a few of us, it becomes (or has become) an obsession. For those of us obsessed it's not just about catching fish, it's the whole experience. The day I find myself upset over getting skunked is the day I need to quit. I know that day will never come.

I've put together in writing my lifetime of experience, the knowledge gained from those experiences, and lessons learned from speaking with countless others about their experiences. My goal was to write a single book that has all the information you need for both salmon and steelhead when fishing the rivers and streams of this beautiful planet. By following the guidelines in the pages that follow you *will* become a better fisherman.

As we know nothing beats actual time on the water for learning how to fish. You can learn so much just by being out there and experiencing it for yourself. That being said, the better prepared you are, the better fisherman you'll become. This book is not only for the beginner but for anglers of all levels. We can all learn from the content found herein. For those of you that have salmon and steelhead fishing experience under your belt, this book should help you get to the next level. Myself and all the experts I'm fortunate to know all say the same thing, we continue to learn at this sport we love and are always striving to get better.

Back in the 1970's when I began steelhead fishing it was normal for most rivers in Washington to have several thousand salmon and steelhead return each year, with many rivers into double-digit thousands of returning fish. Back then if you caught your limit it was considered good, in fact excellent. It still is. Now that some runs are depressed and the numbers of fish returning to their natal rivers are often counted in the hundreds rather than the thousands, catching even a single (or few) salmon or steelhead is excellent...your limit, well that's fantastic.

But the good news is that even under adverse run conditions, if you're armed with the knowledge of proper techniques, and then use them to your advantage, it is still possible to experience days where the number of steelhead or salmon hooked can be in the double digits. You may find this hard to believe, but trust me, it's true!

Will this book help you achieve that level of expertise? Well, that depends to a great extent upon you. All of the information necessary to become a highly skilled salmon and steelhead angler is contained within the pages of this book. If you follow the precepts found herein and devote the necessary time to applying them on the river, you most certainly will become a better fisherman.

Please enjoy and we'll see you on the river.

Chapter 1
STEELHEAD AND SALMON: THE FISH

Epic steelhead.

A steelhead is a sea-run rainbow trout (anadromous; *Oncorhynchus mykiss*) usually returning to freshwater to spawn after two to three years at sea. Steelhead are a species of salmonid native to tributaries of the Pacific Ocean and the great Northwest. They have also been introduced to the Great Lakes area and are very popular among fishermen in that region.

Steelhead are considered one of the hardest species to catch and are prized by anglers throughout the world. Beginners can spend countless hours and days on the river without even having a bite (or not realizing they had a bite). As knowledge is gained and experience increases, so will the catch rate. This book will help you with the learning curve and hopefully cut those hours and days down to a minimum. As you progress with your knowledge, success will come.

Winter Steelhead
Winter steelhead make up the bulk of steelhead fishing. Winter and steelhead are pretty much synonymous with most fishermen.

Generally speaking, from mid November through April there are rivers up and down the West Coast that will have steelhead running in them.

Hatchery steelhead start entering coastal Washington rivers in mid November, although December is usually known as the beginning of winter steelhead season for California, Oregon, British Columbia and the Puget Sound area rivers in Washington. The hatchery season generally lasts through February, or as late as May in rivers that have broodstock programs.

In Washington the adipose fin is removed from smolts before they are released into the rivers. A missing adipose fin with a healed-over scar indicates the fish was raised in a hatchery and is available to catch and keep when the season allows. Some hatcheries, primarily tribal, clip a ventral fin instead of the adipose. As always, it's a must to read the regulations and know them prior to fishing in any river for any species.

Because hatchery smolts are released as early as possible into the rivers to "footprint" them, they also return earlier than wild (or native) fish that are born in the river itself.

8

Hatchery fish are no longer viewed as the "cookie cutter" fish of years past, due in large part to the implementation of brood-stock programs on many rivers. Most broodstock programs use native breeding pairs to produce offspring with the same genes as their native parents, but the juvenile fish are then reared in a hatchery environment. Usually only the largest and healthiest native fish are used for breeding in an effort to create strong, healthy fish with a better chance to survive and return in both greater number and size.

Although still considered hatchery fish, unlike their cousins of typical hatchery origin which tend to show up early in the run, these fish usually return later in the run during the same time period that native fish begin to show up. This allows anglers the opportunity to harvest a fish during a time when the weather and water conditions are more conducive to the average fisherman.

Hatchery steelhead can be willing biters if a bait is presented in a natural looking manner, and once an angler hooks a steelhead, whether it be of hatchery, broodstock or wild origin, they themselves usually become hooked for life. Regardless of lineage, these fish are all steelhead, and having overcome the ridiculous odds of survival in the ocean to make it back to this point, they are not about to give up easily and fight with everything they have.

Native, or "wild", steelhead should all be considered trophy fish and gently released back into the river so they can reproduce and breed for generations to come. Not to say I don't target them, but I respect them and hope that everyone that reads this book does as well.

In most states and British Columbia it has finally become law that wild fish are not allowed to be retained. These are some of the most spectacular fish you'll ever see. Wild not only describes their existence, but also how fierce they can be. Pound for pound you will not find a harder fighting fish.

Wild fish start trickling into the rivers during late January and February, but the majority enter even later in February, March and even into April.

More spots, more color and ferocious fighters, wild steelhead are generally a little bigger than hatchery fish, about 8 to 10 pounds. But, true trophy fish over 20 pounds can be hooked. A 20-pound steelhead is often referred to as a trophy, but a steelhead in the teens is something to behold. You'll also notice the majority of so-called 20-pound fish are not even close to actually being 20 pounds, because most fishermen have no clue how big a 20-pound fish actually is.

The Skeena Region of British Columbia and the Olympic Peninsula in Washington are still world-class fisheries that produce many 20-pound fish each year.

In some areas fewer and fewer native fish are returning each year so, again, please respect these fish and treat them accordingly. A picture says a thousand words and makes a much better statement than a fish in the freezer.

Spring Steelhead

Yes, there are actually spring steelhead. Not common at all, there are very few areas that offer a true spring run, most notably the Skeena Region in British Columbia and a few rivers on the Olympic Peninsula.

Just as spring chinook, "springers", are the hardest fighting salmon, so too are spring steelhead the toughest and most beautiful of the steelhead species. Absolutely gorgeous and having no "give up" in their blood, these are true native fish and come just

The Skeena region holds some remarkable spring steelhead.

GIL MCKEAN

Mike Perusse with a summer steelhead.

prior to the summer run. April and May are the best months for these fish and are generally found close to the ocean. They are in and out of the river system very quickly, having spawned within weeks of entering fresh water.

These are prized fish and very few fishermen even realize they exist; even fewer have ever battled with one.

Summer Steelhead

Summer steelhead can provide for some of the most comfortable and memorable fishing of the year. Because water conditions are typically lower and clearer during this period, lighter tackle is often employed, making the battle even more challenging. The fish themselves, being cold blooded creatures, are generally more active in the warmer flows and can become quite territorial when the water drops, often striking with a vengeance and then "tailwalking" across the water's surface, putting on a spectacle not soon forgotten.

Summer steelhead returns can number in the hundreds of thousands on some river systems. Some of the more popular summer steelhead systems in the Northwest include the Trinity River in California, Rogue and Umpqua rivers in Oregon, the Columbia River system and its tributaries which span Oregon, Washington and Idaho, and the Skeena River system in British Columbia. Numerous smaller coastal and inland rivers support runs of summer steelhead as well.

When river levels drop and clear, these summer fish can often be found in riffles and pocket water taking advantage of the higher oxygen levels found there. They may also feel more secure due to the surface being obscured by the faster-moving water. Hooking a big fish in this skinny water is a surefire recipe for a spectacular fight as the fish has limited maneuvering room and typically either jumps straight up, or makes a sizzling run for deeper water—or both!

Summer fish typically begin returning to their natal rivers as early as May and can be fished for throughout the summer months and well into fall. Some rivers, such as Oregon's Mackenzie and Deschutes, have runs of chinook salmon that coincide with returning summer steelhead allowing anglers to fish for both species simultaneously.

Many rivers have returns of both hatchery and wild summer steelhead, and care should be taken during the hottest part of the season as the mortality rate of fish hooked and played in extremely warm conditions goes up exponentially. Early mornings are often a good time to chase summer steelhead, owing to the fact that water temperatures often cool during the night. The combination of pleasant weather conditions and the more active nature of summer-run steelhead makes this a great time of year to get out there and catch some of these spectacular fish!

Chinook Salmon

Chinook (*Oncorhynchus tshawytscha*) are the largest species in the salmon family and probably the most popular among fishermen. They are also known as king salmon, spring salmon and Tyee salmon, especially by our Canadian brothers. Chinook are native to the North Pacific Ocean and the river systems of western North America ranging from California to Alaska. They are also native to Asia. Just like steelhead, they have also been introduced to the Great Lakes area and are extremely popular amongst fishermen.

Chinook are blue-green on the back and top of the head with silvery sides and white ventral surfaces. Often you'll notice a purple hue, especially when they are in shallow water or freshly out of the water. They have black spots on their tail and upper half of their body.

Chinook salmon generally spend 4 years in the ocean before returning to their home rivers to spawn, however some will return in just one or two years. These fish are referred to as "jacks" and are significantly smaller than their more mature brethren. The average adult chinook usually weighs in the teens, but there are some fish that wait 5, 6 and even 7 or 8 years to return to spawn—these will be the 30-plus-pound fish we dream of. Chinook spawn in larger and deeper waters than other salmon species and can be found on the spawning redds (nests) from September through to December.

One *Seattle Times* article states, "Pacific salmon have disappeared from 40 percent of their historic range outside Alaska," and concludes that it is imperative that people realize the needs of salmon and try not to contribute to destructive practices that harm salmon runs.

Just like with steelhead, we need to respect these fish and only harvest what we really think we need. Hatchery fish are intended for harvest, so wild fish should be released as a gesture of respect. Some of the most beautiful photos I have are of chinook salmon I have released.

Releasing a chunky chinook.

Springers

True spring-run chinook salmon are among the most prized fish for their table fare and hard-nosed fighting style. Usually running from March through May they have a large buildup of fat, are very eager to bite and are full of fight. Although averaging around 15 pounds, many are hooked each year in the mid to upper 20-pound range.

Spring chinook enter river systems when waters are cold and full of oxygen which warrants no restrictions on travel. With this in mind, spring chinook are found travelling in shallow water, about 9 to 25 feet in depth in larger river systems such as the Columbia River, and along the banks on most others. In order to make travel as easy as possible, spring chinook dodge heavy head-on currents by travelling the river edges where the speed of the flow is reduced.

The highly prized springer.

Coho Salmon

Coho salmon (*Oncorhynchus kisutcho*) are commonly known as silver salmon or "silvers". Coho have silver sides and dark blue backs. Many changes take effect when coho enter the rivers to begin their spawning phase. Both males and females begin by darkening up and their sides begin to turn red. Most notably the male tends to get an unusual characteristic that most anglers notice: a hooked nose. Both males and females darken and have a red hue. The hook is more pronounced in the males but it does occur on females as well.

Males also develop a slight hump on the shoulders when ready to spawn.

Jacks come back in 2 years to spawn, with the adults coming back in 3 or 4 years. It's usually the 4 year olds that develop this "hook" and can weigh in the teens, although the majority will be around 8-10 pounds. Any coho over 20 pounds should be considered a trophy.

Coho fishing is extremely popular in the Northwest and Canada and is gaining in popularity every year due to their wild acrobatics and drag-spooling abilities.

A hook nosed coho.

(Top left) Tiffany Pott is all smiles with this nice pink salmon.
(Bottom left) Debbie Turner with a nice summer steelhead.
(Top right) Bryanna Zimmerman with a hatchery steelhead
(notice the dorsal fin).
(Top center) The author with a male (buck) steelhead.
(Bottom right) A river caught sockeye salmon.

Big ol' chum salmon.

Chum Salmon

Chum Salmon (*Oncorhynchus keta*) are also known as dog salmon or Keta salmon. Although it has nothing to do with its name, I like to think that it's because they fight like a dog that they ended up with the nickname of "dog" salmon. Chum are one of the hardest-fighting salmon in the rivers and believe me, it is a dog fight!

While in the salt or just entering a river, chum are chrome bright and sometimes hard to distinguish from other species. They are, however, usually characterized by the purple blotchy streaks running down their sides when returning to spawn in the rivers. Spawning males typically grow an elongated nose, their teeth become increasingly pronounced and are just plain mean looking.

Chum are usually the last salmon to spawn (November to January); they are very territorial and protect their redds. Most chum redds are found in the tailouts of large holes or in flats. Chum are very aggressive and will fight with all they have.

Pink Salmon

Pink salmon (*Oncorhynchusgorbuscha*), also known as humpies, are the smallest and most abundant of the salmon species. On odd-numbered years, they return in the millions to certain rivers in the Pacific Northwest. Alaska and Canada receive runs every year.

Pink salmon return when they're two years old and generally only reach between 3 and 6 pounds. Males form a large "hump" on their back, thus the nickname.

A common misconception about pink salmon is their lack of fighting ability. This is largely because given "normal" salmon gear they don't put up a huge fight. But use ultra-light gear, basically a trout rod, spinning reel and 6-pound line and you'll have more than enough fight to keep you hooting and hollering all day. More and more these fish are becoming a popular choice among fishermen for their ease of catching. It's not uncommon to have double-digit days of catch and release for these fish, and using the proper techniques these days should be the norm.

Sockeye Salmon

Sockeye salmon (*Oncorhynchus nerka*) are also called red salmon, especially in Alaska. There is also a landlocked version of sockeye known as kokanee.

Known for their deep red flesh, sockeye are widely considered the best table fare amongst all the salmon species.

Sockeye spawn best in rivers that have a freshwater lake associated with them. The fry stay in the lake up to a couple of years before migrating out to the ocean, returning in 2 to 4 years, the majority as 4 year olds. On river systems that do not have a lake they usually return to the river system sooner, in 1 to 4 years, the majority being 2 and 3 year olds.

For those who have fished for sockeye in freshwater lakes there is a misconception that sockeye do not fight. This couldn't be further from the truth and, in fact, can be one of the hardest-fighting fish prior to their spawning state. By the time these fish enter freshwater lakes, they have begun breaking down and don't have the oxygen necessary to put up a good fight. Hook one of these fish straight from the ocean on a fresh stream and they'll give you all the fight you need.

Sockeye only eat plankton, which can make it difficult to figure out how to catch them, but don't worry, we've found ways and I will share the secrets of hooking these gorgeous fish in the pages to follow.

Chapter 2

PREPARING TO FISH

A little cold out.

Regulations

Being prepared can be just as important, if not more important, than the fishing itself when looking for a successful outing. It goes without saying that you should have your fishing license, catch record cards and appropriate endorsements, but you'd be surprised how many anglers are cited each year for lack of the proper credentials.

Regulations are meant to be followed but can be tough to decipher. It's always best to read the regulations in advance to make sure of open times, bait restrictions, gear restrictions and possession limits. Each state, or in Canada's case province, has their own set of regulations. I carry a copy with me in my backpack for reference. Then, if I decide to change rivers in the middle of a trip, I will have easy access to the regulations for that area. There are

many circumstances when having a copy with you will come in handy. Regulations should also be available online for those of you that are computer savvy. This can be a quicker option, using the search feature to go directly to the subject you're inquiring about.

The one regulation we see being violated time after time is snagging. I don't understand the reasoning of those that feel this is fishing. In fact in the Great Lakes area they have their own name for snaggers—Loogans. Don't be a Loogan!

Historic Records

Record keeping is a vital part of knowing when to fish and for what species. This can be your own records or those that are kept by the Department of Fisheries in each state or province. While most of the information you're looking for will be available online from each State, some of the more detailed information should be written in your own journal.

All those that are serious about fishing should keep a journal. There are more advanced online journals you can purchase on the web that will offer more fields than you'd ever want to fill out and many of these have a place for pictures as well, but even a hand-written journal is better than none. As we get older we sometimes forget the details or dates about certain runs so this is a way to refresh our memory and show trends.

Those records available from the Department of Fisheries should include smolt releases and reported catch records from each river, or each species. Catch records will show you how many of each species are caught each month, a good way to plan what rivers to consider during a certain time period. Also look at the run forecasts for each river and species. Although not always accurate at least they give you an indication of what to expect in the upcoming season.

Weather/River Levels

Salmon and steelhead fishermen should be prepared for any kind of weather. Rain, snow, ice, wind, it doesn't matter. Well, maybe it does. We'll fish in any weather but will the river be fishable when we get to it?

In order for a river to be fishable it does need to have some visibility and the flow needs to be that where a fish will be comfortable enough to strike your presentation. Weather is the main reason why visibility and flow conditions change, except for those

(Top right) Be respectful of the water.
(Middle right) Tying jigs and doing homework on the Internet.
(Bottom) Doing your homework pays off.

MIKE ZAVADLOV

GIL MCKEAN

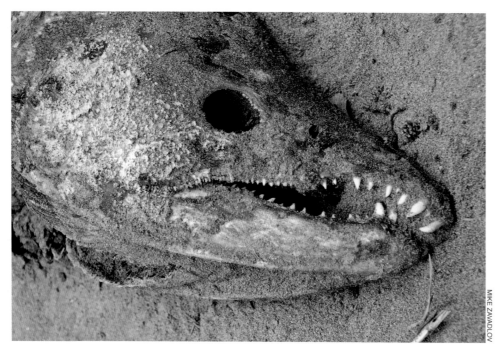

End of the cycle.

rivers that are controlled by a dam. Rain will also bring color to a river. Think of all the foreign material that is brought into a river by water runoff. Some color is good, in fact some color can be great because it provides a feeling of protection for the fish. But too much color might make it difficult for the fish to see your presentation. Rain also affects the flow. The more rain, the more runoff, the faster the flow. Pretty simple thinking here.

So does that mean when it rains we shouldn't go? Absolutely not! Rain in general is a good thing. Rain will bring fresh fish into the river systems. What we have to watch for is too much rain, which might put a river into a flood stage.

You should always check the river height and flow a few days prior to your outing and monitor it all the way up to your departure. There are online resources available for most rivers, but for those rivers that don't have a gauge, look for other rivers in close proximity and that should be a good enough indication. Most sites that monitor flows will have a median flow which indicates what normal river conditions look like. By following the graph you can determine if the river is holding steady, rising or falling. Although it's impossible to always have the perfect situation, a falling river will more often than not be the best fishing. A rising river is not the preferred situation, but again we cannot always choose the conditions in which we are about to fish.

Following the weather forecast is a good way to predict what the river will be like on the dates you choose to fish. If rain is forecast, how much? Has it been raining for a week or is it just a single day? A good rain after many rainless days is usually a good thing. A good rain after many days of rain, well, the river might already be out of shape. Look at the flows again and see what the graph says.

Temperature can also play an important role in both river color and flow. Freezing weather will stop the flow of smaller creeks and runoff into the main body of water thus clearing up the water. As the weather warms, ice and snow melt and more runoff can be expected. With more runoff comes more color and more flow. If the main body of water is very colored up, look for clear water entering the system from smaller creeks. It's very common for salmon and steelhead to seek this fresh, clean water and the bite could be phenomenal.

By following the weather, flows and height you should be comfortable in knowing if the river is going to be fishable or not.

Hi-Tech Communications

Before the Internet I don't know how many trips were wasted by arriving at a river and finding it washed out. Most of those trips can be avoided now that we have all the tools available for weather and river conditions, but the Internet offers us so much more.

Fish reports are all over the Internet; the trick is to know which ones to trust. Places like Steelhead University and Salmon University have actual reports from guides that submit their information, which has been screened to make sure the data they provide is accurate and not just an advertising ploy to get more clients.

There are all kinds of fishing Boards or Forums which can contain a wealth of information, but keep in mind that anyone

Buzz Ramsey is a big believer in keeping a journal.

The end of a successful day.

can post on these boards and the information is not verified. It's not uncommon for someone to post a great report on a river in the hope that people will go there and bypass the river the person actually intends to fish. Also common are bad reports on a river that is on fire, again hoping people will bypass the river and leave more room for the person posting. It doesn't take long to figure out which people have accurate posts and which are trying to brag or steer you in the wrong direction. Once you figure out who you can trust, these can become a valuable resource.

Social networking is all the rage these days and another great source for information. Facebook and Twitter being the two main players; get a free account and "friend", "like", or "follow" those that are in the know. As the people that post are targeting their family, friends and followers, this information tends to be more accurate than the forums. This is also a great venue to ask questions. Make it a private message if you don't want everyone to see. You'll find most anglers are more than willing to help out a fellow fisherman.

The Internet is also a great place to explore new rivers that you want to fish. One of the places I like to frequent is Google Earth. This will show a full view of the river from space and you can zoom in to get the details. Not the same thing as being on the water and experiencing it, but for finding new rivers you'll be able to see put-ins, take-outs, bends, rapids and logjams. Note that these views are usually a few months behind so always be prepared for new hazards not shown online.

Cell phones are a great way to communicate, but smart phones are the way to go. Just think, not only can you talk to or text your buddies and get up-to-the-minute reports, but you can access the Internet for all the information above. Use it as a GPS, get current weather and river flows, access your journal, take a picture if your camera is in your backpack (or maybe fell in the river, yes it's happened to me a few times), or even use it as a flashlight in an emergency. There are tons of fishing apps available, just explore and you'll find some that will be beneficial to you.

Chapter 3

HARDWARE

Calvin Sampson putting a hurting on a fall chinook.

Terminal Tackle

Hooks

Those who fish with me know that I'm anal about my hooks. They must be ultra-sharp and ultra-strong, or I don't use them...simple as that. With today's technology in manufacturing, we are very fortunate that premium hooks come factory sharpened with names like needle point, cutting point, laser point, surgically sharpened and others. These premium hooks do come with a premium price compared to standard hooks, generally around $0.20 apiece compared to maybe $0.03 apiece for those that are not precision sharpened and tempered. Now if you're like me you're thinking, ah, that's nothing. But you'd be surprised at the amount of people that won't spend almost a quarter per hook. For me there's no compromise, I want a hook that's going to stick and hold...period.

Size of hooks will depend on method used and what species we're targeting.

Steelhead
• Drift Fishing: Size 4, 2 or 1
• Side Drifting: Size 4 double-hook setup or size 2 single hook
• Float-Fishing: Size 1 to 2/0
• Spinners/Spoons: Size 1/0 to 2/0
• Plugs: Size 2/0 to 3/0

Salmon
• Drift Fishing: Size 1/0, 2/0 (pinks, coho), Size 2/0 to 3/0 (coho, chum, chinook)
• Float-Fishing: Size 1/0 to 3/0
• Spinners/Spoons: Size 2/0 to 3/0
• Plugs: Size 3/0 to 4/0 (larger chinook)

These are only generalizations and you can use smaller or larger depending on the situation. In clear water we tend to use the smallest gear we can get away with; dirtied-up water, the opposite without going too large.

You'll also want to make sure your lure or bait isn't so large that it gets in the way of "hooking" the fish.

Swivels

Swivels are a viable part of the complete setup but thank goodness only barrel swivels are required in most cases instead of snap or coast lock swivels which can really put a strain on the wallet. I like good strong ball-bearing swivels, but I usually only use the smallest barrel swivels I trust to put a tension release point between the presentation and the main line. Different manufacturers have different sizes and ratings, and I usually have a good supply of those rated from 20 pounds up to 65 pounds.

As with hooks, I try to get away with the smallest hardware I can. I prefer black so it's not seen as well in the water. Stainless or chrome can actually attract the fish, but we want the fish to attack our presentation, not the swivel, although this does happen on occasion. Funny, but they don't stick this way.

Weight

Weight is an important factor when it comes to hooking fish, in fact, very important. You'll want to remember that the majority of salmon and steelhead are found within 2 feet of the bottom. This is extremely critical with steelhead. Salmon can be hooked throughout the water column but, by far, the majority will be found within the bottom 2 feet.

Finding the bottom is easy but what can be difficult is getting your presentation within that 2-foot window while maintaining a natural presentation. Too much weight and it will drag and not look natural. Obviously, with too little weight you won't even be near the bottom.

A good rule of thumb when drifting is that you want your weight to "tick" the bottom about every 3 to 5 seconds. This way you know your presentation is right near the bottom, but not dragging in an unnatural way.

Good old fashioned pencil lead is still what the majority of us use. It's flexible, easy to use and highly adjustable (a good pair of dykes helps here). Start off with too much lead and it's simple to nip some off the end until you get that perfect drift. Not enough? Put it back and grab a new piece.

I like to attach my lead by leaving a long tag end in the knot from the main line to the swivel, and then slip some hollow-core pencil lead over the tag and crimp it down. If it becomes hung up it can be pulled off the tag before it breaks your line. If you lose the lead it only takes a few seconds to reapply a new one. Again, trimming the end will allow you to reach that perfect drift.

When float-fishing for salmon, I'll use the same setup: a long tag end and pencil lead. For steelhead I prefer an inline weight. Since inline weights are specified by size it's easy to calculate the size of the float necessary to maintain that perfect natural drift. Weight + lure weight = Float Weight. For example: 1/4-ounce inline weight plus a 1/8-ounce jig = 3/8-ounce float.

Another popular drifting weight is a piece of parachute cord with BB-shot inside. These Slinky drift weights, as they are known, can be purchased ready-to-fish from the tackle shops, or they can be made at home. They can be made or purchased in various lengths and weights to match the fishing conditions.

Sometimes if you need just a tad bit more weight when drifting or floating, a simple split shot or two will do. Easy on, easy off. They're a simple solution to getting that balance you're looking for.

Floats

There are so many different kinds of floats, and a lot of it comes down to personal preference. Balsa, Styrofoam, foam, cork, plastic—they're all good as long as the drift is natural.

The thinner-diameter floats are used more for smaller water where you don't want the current to push your float too fast. Thicker-diameter floats are great for large water, and the larger baits primarily used for salmon. Experiment with floats to determine which type you like best.

Generally speaking I don't use more than a 1/2-ounce float for steelhead and my "go to" size would be 3/8 ounce. But when it comes to salmon fishing I use the big boys made out of foam.

These may reach a couple ounces but if that's what it takes given the weight, depth of the hole and current to get the presentation down near the bottom, than that's what I'll use.

Most of my floats are black on the bottom end for stealth. Natural balsa also looks good, and then there is the clear float. Whatever you feel is the stealthiest would be your best bet.

Most floats have a body color and then two stripes on the top. The bottom stripe should be about even with the surface of the water in order to float properly. The top stripe is your site indicator. Make sure you can see the color against the surroundings. Fluorescent red is the most popular color, but fluorescent orange and chartreuse work well too. The fish can't see the top of the float but make sure you can!

Rods

As with everything else, rods have come a long way. My first "steelhead" rod was a Fenwick Fiberglass rod rated 8-17 pounds. It was 8 1/2 feet long and was probably 3/4 of an inch in diameter near the butt. What a fantastic rod...at the time.

After a few years I was able to save enough money to purchase my first "graphite" rod. Wow, was this cool! 8 1/2 feet long, rated 8-12 pounds and thinner than I'd ever seen before in a steelhead rod. With graphite came sensitivity, and with sensitivity came fish. But with graphite also came a brittle rod, and on my third trip out to Reiter Ponds I was greeted with a loud snap on my first cast of the morning. Heartbreaking, to say the least.

Luckily I was making $2.85 an hour at the time so it didn't take long to save up for my next great rod, a Lamiglas 9' graphite rod rated 8-12 pounds. That was in 1979 and I still have that rod!

Jump forward 30 years to where we are today and the choices are endless. Now I'm not saying that a more expensive rod will

Ready to swim back.

STEVE TURNER

Float it!

catch more fish, but if you can feel more, well…you would tend to think you would hook more.

The more expensive rods all have one thing in common—sensitivity. The new materials being used are not only more sensitive, but stronger too. You'll notice that a top-of-the-line rod built in 1979 and rated at 8-12 pounds will be much thicker than that same rod built with today's technology. I like to "feel" everything on the bottom and these new rods let you do just that…for a price.

For the upper-end rods—G. Loomis, Fetha Styx, Lamiglas—you're going to spend $300+ for a good drift rod. My suggestion if your budget is limited would be to spend all that you can afford on a quality rod as this will serve you well and help you feel and thus hook more fish. Will cheaper rods catch fish? Of course, but you may end up wondering how many fish you didn't feel.

With so many choices, here is a good guideline for selecting the proper rod; consult with a reputable sporting goods dealer or manufacturer and ask specific questions in order to determine which rod is best suited to your needs and budget.

No single rod will do everything. I have over 30 rods and use them all, although I do have my favorites.

Drift Fishing
• Steelhead: 9'; 8-12-pound rating; fast action
• Salmon: 10': 10-20-pound rating; fast action

Side Drifting
• Steelhead: 9' 6"; 4-8-pound rating; slow action
• Salmon: 10'; 6-12-pound rating; slow action

Float-Fishing
• Steelhead: 10' 6"; 6-10-pound rating; moderate action
• Salmon: 10' 6"; 10-20-pound rating; moderate action

Reels
Along with rods comes a properly matched reel. Everyone has their favorite type: bait-caster, spinning or center-pin and they're all good and have their own advantages. Best thing I can say here is go with a reel that has the best drag system (except center-pins, which have none) and that you're comfortable with.

When I first started steelhead fishing I was using a spinning reel. It was a couple years later that I finally got my skills up enough to graduate to a bait-caster. Never again would I use a spinning reel, as that's for beginners. Or so I thought.

That was then, now I can honestly say I use spinning reels more than bait-casters for steelhead, although for salmon I still use bait-casters.

For almost every method you can use either a bait-caster or a spinning reel, and while each may have its advantages, it really just comes down to personal preference.

Drift Fishing
It used to be like I described above, you actually weren't truly drift fishing until you could use a bait-caster. Of course along with the bait-caster came bird's nests and frustration. Once mastered though, you could see the benefits—accurate casting, power and a great drag system. You could also control the cast and/or the drag with your thumb (hence the saying, "thumbing it").

MIKE ZAVADLOV

MIKE PERUSSE

BILL HERZOG

(Top left) The author fishing the center-pin.
(Center left) Be flexible. Both baitcasters and spinning rigs were used for this limit.
(Bottom left) A measuring tape is handy when determining weight.
(Top right) Enjoy the beauty.
(Bottom right) A well setup Mike Perusse.

Spinning reels are preferred while side drifting.

Today the bait-caster is still preferred by the majority of drift fishermen, but nobody thinks the guy fishing with the spinning reel is a novice anymore. Spinning reels have come so far that they actually have great drag systems now. A spinning reel would be preferred for super-light setups where ultra-light presentations are required on small water.

I recommend a bait-caster in size 100 to 200 for steelhead, and size 200 to 300 for salmon. A spinning reel in size 2500 works well for both species.

Float-Fishing

I have my own preferences for float-fishing, but again, it's all personal preference. Under most circumstances I prefer a spinning reel when float-fishing for steelhead. You can cast plenty far with lighter floats and presentations, and with the bail open you can control how much line comes off the reel without causing unnecessary drag. As mentioned above, the drag systems on new spinning reels are fantastic so you don't have to worry about a fish spooling you or a hot fish burning up your drag.

For salmon I prefer a bait-caster. Much heavier presentations, along with heavier fish, require more control of the fish once hooked. With the heavier presentation the line rolls off the reel when the spool is disengaged. For beginners, make sure you adjust your casting tension so you don't end up with a nasty bird's nest, which sometimes necessitates cutting most, if not all, of your line off in order to rectify the situation.

The Importance of a Good Drag System

Example 1

A few years back I was fishing on the Humptulips River with my friend Phil Stephens, one of the best guides around. Phil had just received his order of new rods and reels for the upcoming salmon season. The bait-casters he received were new to him so we decided to give them a good workout before he let clients use them. They cast great and reeled in smoothly, but when it came to fighting fish, let's just say we not only broke them in, we actually broke them.

You see, there is a difference between a 20-pound chinook on the end of the line and a 50-plus-pounder. This was the first 50-pound salmon I had ever hooked and it was a monster. After one look at the boat it had seen enough and decided to high-tail it down river. The sheer awesome power of this fish was unbelievable. But then the new reel went from singing to surging, to a big 'ol sa nap! Phil looked at me in disbelief,

"Holy crap, you thumbed it!" he said.

"Ah, no, when have you ever seen me thumb a fish like that?" I said.

The expletives started flying and I was laughing as I tried to say it was no big deal, we'll catch another. But that wasn't the point, what if I had been one of his customers? A 50-pound fish would have done wonders for his business.

As it turns out we opened the side plate of the reel and the parts simply fell out. The gears and drag system had literally exploded.

Phil was on the phone immediately with the reel representative and told him to come pick up the reels; they weren't going to work out.

Phil has never used that brand again, nor will I.

Example 2

In 2011 I was back to fish the Nushagak River in Alaska for the third year in a row. Having fished it before, I knew how strong these fish were and how many we might catch—100-plus in a day between three guys was a definite possibility and a goal we sought to achieve. I had Jeff Norwood and Terry Fors along with me for this trip, both excellent fishermen, and we worked flawlessly as a team trying for that magical 100-fish day.

Long story short, between the three of us we hooked and landed 175 chinook salmon one day and 191 the next! Those were two days that produced numbers I probably won't see again. We set camp records that will be hard to top. (100-fish days are not common and should not be expected. The average day from 2009-2011 was 37 fish for our boat).

As you would imagine with that many hot king salmon averaging around 20 pounds each and coming straight out of Bristol Bay, a massive amount of stress was put on our gear, especially our drag systems.

Jeff and I used our own gear, high-quality rods and reels. Fors decided to use camp gear that was, well, camp gear. The camp gear was decent but the reels would have their drags replaced a couple times per season. It wasn't 100 fish into the first day and Fors reel blew up. Luckily an extra camp reel was in the boat and we continued fishing. That one was also toast before the end of the day. Fors went through 3 reels (and a rod) while Jeff's and my gear was still working smooth as silk.

You may pay a little extra for a good reel, but it's very well worth it if you intend to use it and not let it sit around and collect dust.

Center-Pin

The center-pin is the ultimate float reel for salmon or steelhead. With no drag and a 1 to 1 retrieve ratio, this is the hardest of all reels to master. Once you have control of it though there's no other experience like it. Casting can be difficult but it is also beautiful when you see it done correctly. The float itself is spectacular. The line flows off the reel from the drift with effortless motion. Nothing could be more natural except for something floating down the river unattached to anything. There is no better way to present your offering to either salmon or steelhead.

Center-pins look pretty simple, but in fact have the most precise engineering design of all the reels and are machined to perfection. This of course, comes at a price, and you can expect to pay between $300 and $500 for a higher end piece of equipment. You will find that there is a difference between the low and high-end reels at this level. If you want to get into this game, I recommend that you borrow or use a reel prior to purchasing one. It will be a mighty expensive experiment if you decide center-pinning isn't for you.

Line

Wow, talk about choices. So much has changed and so much has gotten better it's unbelievable. Mono, co-polymer, fluorocarbon, braid, fusion…what's next?

Monofilament

Easily the most common form of fishing line and what almost all anglers use at some point. Mono, as it's referred to, is made from plastic and has stretch to it. The stretch can be a benefit when

Float fishing has also brought back the popularity of the spinning reel.

The center-pin and chrome—a natural combination.

using lighter line as it has "give" before it reaches its breaking point. The more line that is off the reel, the more stretch you will have.

Although line ratings are supposed to be uniform, all manufacturers seem to have a different spec sheet. The best way to find the correct line is try it yourself. It's the least expensive of the lines and regular replacement is advised. I like to stay with a neutral color for most applications, either clear or green.

Co-Polymer

The so-called mono replacement is co-polymer fishing line. Instead of a single strand (mono) it has two or more strands. There is slightly less stretch with co-polymer, but there is a little stretch so as not to shock the hook when setting it. Another plus is less memory which is particularly beneficial with spinning reels. Less memory equates to better casting. Small nicks may lead to breakage with mono, but because of the multiple strands you are less likely to break with co-polymer. The one major drawback of copolymer is that it's thicker than the other lines.

Fluorocarbon

I can talk about all the scientific terms that make up fluorocarbon line, but what we really need to know is that it is nearly invisible under water. The line was developed in Japan as a method to trick the finicky fish of Asia. Now fluorocarbon is in common use

The author navigating some rapids.

worldwide, especially for leaders. Getting the line wet prior to securing a knot is a must so you don't "burn" the line and weaken it. It has very little to no stretch. Although some spool their reels with this line, I recommend using it only as leader material.

Braid/Fusion

When I mention braid in the salmon and steelhead world I'm specifically talking about spectra braid. Extremely strong and thin, it also has the natural ability to float. Braid is very popular with float-anglers as 30-pound braid is the equivalent diameter of 8-pound-diameter mono. It's also extremely sensitive and in combination with a sensitive rod it is as if you can feel every bump on the bottom. The one drawback of braid is zero stretch. A couple ways to compensate for lack of stretch would be:

    1. A longer moderate to slow-action rod

    2. Tying a section of mono between the leader and the main line, a bumper section (10-20 feet long)

    3. Quit setting the hook like a bass fisherman! A slight, quick upward motion will set the hook.

So why is no stretch bad? For one, it's easy to rip the hook right out of the fish's mouth, but that $300 rod will snap rather easily with such shock force. Sounds like a shotgun.

Fusion is very similar but combines different components to form this line.

Apparel

One thing to consider when fishing is what you're wearing. No, the river is not a place to make a fashion statement, but you do want to remain dry and warm. There's nothing worse than being cold, except being cold and wet. Falling in the river almost always ruins a good day of fishing no matter what you're wearing, but good-quality boots and clothing can minimize the effects of rain, snow, ice and wind.

Waders/Boots

Thirty years ago hip boots were considered the best way to wade in the water and remain safe. Today, not many hip boots are seen on the rivers. Most all fishermen have converted to chest waders and the majority of these waders are "breathable". There are still the holdouts and there's really nothing wrong with hip boots. They do, however, fill up very fast when stepping too deep or falling in. If worn properly with a safety belt around the waist, waders will not fill up with water as quickly and should allow a little more time for an angler to attempt to reach safer ground.

Neoprene waders offer a small amount of buoyancy which can help in a fall, but the main reason for choosing neoprene waders would be warmth—they are much warmer than breathable or rubber waders. The downside is they are harder to move around in and don't breathe, so working up a sweat while walking the river can result in the sweat turning cold and the angler becoming miserable.

Breathable waders are by far the choice of most fishermen. They are the easiest to get around in, lightest material, waterproof and above all…breathable! It does make a difference when the perspiration is allowed to escape, thus keeping you dry inside the waders.

A good pair of fleece pants is recommended under your waders, and on the very cold days possibly even some felt-lined jeans. The waders will keep you dry but you also need to make sure you're warm.

Waders come with a boot foot or a stocking foot. Personal preference again, but I think stocking-foot waders with a good

Sunset on the Nushagak.

pair of wading boots are your best bet. Boot-foot waders tend to be bulkier and don't have that snug feeling or the ankle support you need on slippery rocks.

When looking for a wading boot, get a good-quality boot with good ankle support. The type of sole you choose depends on where you generally fish. For mossy areas you'll want felt soles, and for muddy areas lug soles work best. If you're not sure, a good lug sole with cleats is the best all-around choice.

One word of caution, do not wear felt in the snow or ice. It will stick to the soles when you're out of the water and soon you'll have big ol' clubs of ice on the bottom of your feet making it impossible to walk. Yes, I found this out the hard way.

If you don't want multiple pairs of boots but do want the choices, Korkers make some fantastic boots that have changeable soles to meet your different requirements.

Rain Gear

If nothing else, when it comes to apparel invest in a high-quality wading jacket. A full rain suit is great when you're in a boat, but you can wear a wading jacket in all conditions. In the Pacific Northwest it rains more times than not when we're fishing so make this your top priority. Although there are many fine wading jackets out there, Simms jackets have always protected me from the elements and they stand by their products. Another Pacific Northwest company to consider for those that can't quite pull the trigger on a Simms, is Redington. They make Northwest-quality rain gear at affordable prices.

Gloves

I have a hard time fishing while wearing gloves but I always have a pair with me. Even if I have to stop fishing to warm my hands, having a good pair of gloves is well worth it. While in a pontoon, drift boat or sled, I always put on the gloves while moving or rowing and then take them off to fish.

Hotties hand warmers in each glove also help considerably. I also have Hotties in my pockets to grab while drifting. Many can wear wool gloves or fingerless gloves while fishing and it's worth a try. If it works for you that's great, wear them! If you can't wear them while fishing, make sure you at least have them with you; you'll thank yourself.

Hat

Gotta protect the head and, remember, most body heat escapes from your noggin. A baseball cap works most of the time, but on really cold days put that stocking cap on. Another trick is to wear foam ear plugs on extra cold days; it also helps keep your head warm.

Polarized Sunglasses

Gotta have them...period! Not only to see fish but to see bottom structure, depth, your line, and of course to protect your eyes. I'll wear mine even in the rain if the water is clear. It opens up a whole new world and your success will increase if you know what the structure looks like where you're fishing. Brown or green lenses are good colors for rivers.

Sticky sharp hooks are a must.

Accessories

Knife

There are so many situations in which you might need a knife this should be a given, have a good sharp knife with you at all times. I like to carry a pocket knife in my wading jacket and a good fillet knife in my backpack. For those of you in a pontoon or drift boat, make sure a knife is easily available to you should your anchor get stuck and you start getting pulled down. Cutting the rope might be your only escape.

File

I personally would rather change out a hook than sharpen it. Not everyone thinks like me though and most will want to sharpen their hooks. Have a good, small-toothed file with you and remember to file away from the point.

Pencil/Pen

It's always a good idea to have a pencil or pen around to take notes or to write on a lure. It's also a requirement in some states to have one so you can mark your catch record.

Camera

Ah, pictures... Memories are great but pictures tell the story. Make sure you have your camera with you and keep it protected from the elements. I keep mine in a Pelican crush-proof, waterproof case. Take lots of pictures, but if releasing a fish try to take them quickly so you don't over-stress the fish.

Clippers

Keep a good pair of clippers attached to your wading jacket and always accessible. It's much easier than reaching for the knife, pliers, or as many people do, using your teeth. Use for snipping the tag end off, cutting your line or even trimming yarn.

Pliers

From cutting lead, to pinching a barb, to releasing fish, a good pair of pliers is another "must have" tool and should be well within reach or in your wading jacket.

Flashlight

From traveling in the dark to tying leaders before the sun comes up, a flashlight or headlamp is a must. Make sure the batteries are fresh and you have spare ones as well.

Thermometer

Water temperature can be a good indicator where fish may be holding. Get a thermometer in a case and have it with you in your wading jacket or backpack. It won't take up any space and can be a valuable tool that most anglers don't utilize.

Measuring Tape

Since many of the fish we target will be for catch and release, a fabric measuring tape is a fantastic way of taking quick measurements. You can find these at any craft or sewing store. Make sure you take length and girth measurements in inches. Using the weight formula length X girth squared divided by 775 you can calculate the weight of the fish, and this formula is amazingly accurate. If you don't want to use your calculator, there are many online tools to estimate the weight, given the length and girth.

Backpack

Traveling light is the best way to go when river fishing and sometimes there just isn't enough room to carry it all in your wading jacket or fanny pack. A good-quality waterproof backpack is my choice and carries all the gear I'll ever need for a weekend trip, and then some. Good for carrying those items you don't need all the time, but could. I like to keep beverages, lunch, snacks, camera, flashlight, TP, extra spools and reel, and lots of extra gear that I'll probably never need, but I'll have it just in case.

Tackle Box
Micro tackle boxes work best, and transparent ones are at the top of my list. Try not to overload yourself with too much tackle, but a few micro boxes usually accompany me in my backpack. When jig-, spinner- or spoon-fishing, many times a micro box in my wading jacket is all I'll need for a day's fishing.

Fly Box
To keep flies in? Or how about jigs! A fly box is a great way to keep your jigs organized and ready to rock.

Bait Storage
A bait box on your wading belt is a good way to keep bait readily available. If you're fishing from a boat then your choices are endless, just be sure to keep your bait cool.

Zip-Lock Baggies
A good way to keep things dry, but a great way to bring home fresh roe to cure.

Fish Bag
Large plastic bags work great in the boat or on the river, but a Katch Cooler is preferred for long-term travel or storage. This will keep the fish cool and your vehicle from stinking.

Organization
Admittedly, I am a terrible organizer. It used to be I'd spend a minimum of a couple hours going through my gear, tying leaders, picking which rod and reel, setting out my clothes, waders and boots for a trip the next morning. And I went through this routine time after time. Often I couldn't find what I was looking for. What a waste of time.

Finally, with the help of my wife, we got everything organized and what a difference it makes. Not only does it look cool when you open the garage and half of it makes you feel as if you're in a sporting goods store, but I can get ready in minutes rather than hours and know I have all the right gear with me.

Here are a couple of ideas on getting your gear more organized.

Rods
I mount mine on the ceiling in rod racks. Against a wall is also fine. The trick is to keep them in a sequence you know—by species, length, rating, it doesn't matter as long as you know how to find a rod quickly. I also have all my spinning rods in one area, bait-casters in another. Have the reels already mounted on the rods, spooled-up with a swivel on the end. Even if you don't use the swivel, it will keep the line tight on the spool and keep it from getting tangled. Writing on tape or writing directly on the drywall is also a great way to label each setup, if your other half allows you to do so, that is...

Reels
I like to have my reels spooled with fresh line and ready to go. I also have the spare spools that come with each reel. I try to buy the same model of reels that I like, which is beneficial because I then I have multiple spools that are interchangeable. I have all the spare spools on a shelf in my tackle closet, in rows according to pound test. When I'm ready to go it's easy to grab a couple spare spools and put them in a pocket in my backpack.

Terminal Gear
Oh my, you can never have enough tackle for sure, but the more you have the harder it is to find that perfect size or color you want to take with you. When it comes to beads, corkies, cheaters, swivels, hooks, lead, jigs, spoons, spinners, worms (pink), flies, scents... basically anything and everything that is considered terminal gear, there's nothing better than a plastic storage organizer with see-through bins. The same kind of organizer you see hobbyists use for parts, nuts, bolts, etc. These things are great! I have a 64-drawer organizer with all my smaller stuff and a 44-drawer unit that has larger size bins for some of my bulk supplies.

There's no rule on how to fill them up, but clear bins are a huge bonus when looking for what you want. I also write with a Sharpie on the front of those that are hard to distinguish, such as hook size and brand.

It's amazing how much gear these hold, and empty bins give you another excuse for buying more gear!

Line/Leader
I set aside another shelf in my tackle closet for line. You'll find that when you own multiple reels, the larger bulk-size spools are the way to go. I also have pegs in the closet for hanging leader material, organized by pound test and brand.

Micro Boxes
I've found that having micro tackle boxes with gear specific to the species I'm targeting is a huge advantage. You can get these cheap and then write on each box what species you'll be targeting and which technique. Fill each box with the appropriate gear, then when you're ready to go you'll already have the tackle you need in one or two containers.

After a day or weekend of fishing, replace what tackle you lost with new tackle from your organizers and it's all ready to fish next time.

Just think, no more wondering what to take each time, you've already thought ahead so you can just grab and go.

Waders/Boots/Rain Gear
I have a separate closet in the garage just for my foul-weather and wading gear, complete with hangers and a boot dryer. Hang it up! Not only will it dry better but it will be all ready to go next time out.

Trust me, the more organized you are, the more successful you'll become!

Chapter 4
HOLDING WATER

MIKE ZAVADLOV

Where are they?

Steelhead Holding Water

Yes, it is true that a steelhead has to travel the whole river up to the point of its final destination. Having said that, it doesn't mean the fish is willing to bite in all sections of a river. There's a reason we have "holes" in a river that people name and repeatedly fish; this is holding water. The odds of a steelhead biting in a section of river it is holding in is significantly higher than a section of river it is just cruising through. In fact, usually steelhead will hold in a "hole", then when ready to travel, they won't be on the bite again until the next hole.

Most well-known holes are easy to find; look on the Internet, look for parked cars along the river, tag along with your buddies. We'll discuss reading the water in the next chapter, but first we need to go over the makeup of these so-called holes.

In general, a steelhead hole will be 2 to 8 feet deep, have some sort of protection from predators, be made up of small boulders and have a current speed of roughly that of a fast walk. Simple, right?

Let's try and explain this better by breaking down the parts.

Depth

In general steelhead will hold in water that is between 2 and 8 feet deep. I've caught steelhead in flats that were 1-foot deep and I've also caught steelhead in holes that were a good 15 feet deep. As with everything, this is only a guideline and the majority of fish will be hooked in the holes that have most of the characteristics of the "common" hole.

So why 2 to 8 feet when their cousins, salmon, tend to like deeper holes? Oxygen. Steelhead require more oxygen and they need to have water moving through their gills at all times, either by the current or the fish swimming to maintain a constant flow. While salmon may be found in "frog water", sloughs and DEEP holes, steelhead need the water to be clean, flowing and full of oxygen.

Bottom

The bottom composition ties in directly with depth and the need for oxygen. Ideally, the bottom is made up of boulders of different sizes, from four-man rocks, to basketball-sized boulders, down to fist-sized stones and finally gravel. The water moving over and around these objects creates a break in the current and also produces oxygen. Therefore, you'll find that steelhead like to rest and rebuild their oxygen supply behind the larger rocks.

They also need clean water, which the rocks help filter. A sandy or muddy bottom is out for steelhead no matter how good you think the water looks. Sand or dirt in the gills is an experience steelhead try to avoid.

Protection

When in holding water, steelhead may still be wary of predators, but they want to exert the least amount of energy as possible. Those holes which offer protection, as well as the other characteristics above, are what they're looking for. Protection can come in many different forms: dark shadows, overhangs, undercuts, stumps, fallen trees, large boulders—anything that can help camouflage them from other creatures, mainly man, will increase the odds of a steelhead lurking beneath.

Hole Dissection

Although no two holes look exactly alike, most of your better holes will have three main sections to fish: head, body and tailout.

Head

This is the top of the hole. Usually the hole has a beginning where either riffles or rapids end and the hole begins. The oxygen level is very high here from the rolling water and is a great spot for steelhead to hold before traveling upstream again.

To fish the head section of the river you want your presentation to be fishing when it hits the head, not after it has already passed through. In order to effectively fish the entire head section it's important that you hit either the very top of the head or, better yet, cast above the head and let it flow naturally into the hole. Often as soon as your presentation drops into the hole itself, a steelhead will jump on it.

Body

This, as it sounds, is the main part of the hole. Normally this is the largest section of a hole and is fished the most, whether by choice or accident. The body of the hole is usually calmer than either the head or tailout and most often a little deeper. There is not as much chop or riffles on the surface, but more than likely there is turbulence underneath, which is great because it will move your presentation in a natural state under the water.

Most fishermen mis-fish this section. They will not get their presentation into the head soon enough and then they reel-up before it gets through the tailout. This is especially common when drift fishing.

Tailout

The end of the hole and, in my opinion, the most productive. If you come to a hole and have the river to yourself, attack it from the head down and hit the entire section of the river thoroughly. Oftentimes, however, you don't have the river to yourself and depending on technique, hole size and how others are fishing, you may be limited in your fishing area. I'd fish the tailout over the other two sections in a heartbeat—but again, this is only if you're limited.

The reason you don't want to start at the tailout if the hole is open is you don't want to spook the fish past the hole upriver. By starting at the head and moving down, if the fish are spooked they'll head down to the tailout section, and as you continue to work the hole hopefully they'll become threatened and finally attack your presentation with their predator instinct. Coming to a hole that's already being worked, you're hoping that's already happened; those fishing the head and body have moved fish into the tailout just for you.

As mentioned above, no two holes are exactly alike. When you come to a hole that is exactly as described, you've hit the mother lode. But the reality is that as long as a section of river contains some characteristics of the above-mentioned properties, it should hold fish.

And note that some holes may just be a section behind a rock in the river, maybe 5 feet total. Other holes may actually be a long flat several hundred yards long just loaded with boulders, called a boulder garden. As long as the boulders create oxygen and the fish do not feel threatened, they'll hold fish.

So again, look for the characteristics mentioned above, but don't pass up water just because it doesn't meet all the criteria. The more criteria it does meet, though, the better the chances of it being a killer hole.

Salmon Holding Water

When trying to find the right salmon water you're not going to have to think as much as you will for steelhead. Actually, most species of salmon will let you know where they're at by rolling and jumping, which say, "I'm here, I'm here." Maybe it's not always that obvious, but they do tend to break the water and let their presence be known.

The makeup of a typical salmon hole does not necessarily contain the main ingredients of a steelhead spot—head, body, tailout—but they could. Many times salmon are just looking for a deep slot with some cover.

A nice hatchery chinook.

BRYANNA ZIMMERMAN

(Top) *This hen came from under a tree.*
(Center) *Tidewater salmon.*
(Bottom) *A "Zog Smooch" before release.*

Salmon, not needing as much oxygen as steelhead, are found in different areas where you won't find steelhead, namely deep holes, frog water and sloughs.

Deep Holes

Although salmon will surface or appear just under the surface, there are more salmon near the bottom. Salmon like the deeper, darker holes as they often feel this is all the protection they need. In general, salmon holes start out around 6 feet deep and go to almost 20 feet deep. If you can find a hole in that 8- to 12-foot-deep range, it should be money!

Frog Water

Some of the better coho water is what we call frog water. Huh? Picture water that's barely moving, something you'd picture lily pads and frogs in, that's frog water. This can be found along some flats, around bends or in offshoots of the main river.

Sloughs

As mentioned above, offshoots of the main river. Some sloughs can run back a few yards or a few hundred yards. Don't overlook these areas for salmon, especially coho. They love this stuff. Coho have no problem swimming in them and just milling around for a while. This seems to be a way for them to get out of the current and rest.

Another thing to look for when tracking down salmon holding water is wood. Whether it be sticks, stumps, log jams or trees, wood is good! For some reason, where there is wood in the river you'll find salmon. They love to tuck in this stuff as they must feel it's the ultimate protection. If I see wood structure and there's water between 6 and 20 feet deep, I'm hitting it! And I mean actually hitting it. They'll be right on the wood, so sometimes an offering bouncing off the wood, or as close to the wood as possible, will draw a strike.

As with steelhead, this is only a guideline for what to look for when targeting salmon. Just like steelhead, salmon also must swim through the entire river system to their destination, so it never hurts to try areas that don't "fit the mold."

Canyons and Tide Water

Canyons

These are areas that you won't have to think too hard on. Most canyons are dark and littered with rocks; a good indicator the fish will not be shy. Usually within canyons are spillways or small waterfalls that fish must conquer in order to move upstream to their spawning grounds. They will almost always congregate at the base of the falls, right where the water is tumbling down. One theory is that this is the most oxygen-rich section of the stream so the fish are building themselves up for that next leap to keep their progression moving.

Once they've conquered the leap, they need to rest. So don't go too far. Fish the first flat above the spillway, as they'll tend to rest before moving to the next pool. If there are boulders in the section before the next pool, they'll lay there too, as this will offer them protection as well as build up strength for the next hurdle. You may see fish between the spillway and the base, but more than likely they'll be moving. These areas between pools, unless filled with larger boulders, will not offer the type of water that they feel comfortable holding in. The exception is when there are too many salmon to hold at either end. Then the flats will be stacked with fish too. I've never seen a hole have too many steelhead, but I wouldn't mind it.

Tide Water

When fishing in tide water it's important to understand where you are in the tidal swing. A tide book, newspapers, the Internet and even an app on your smart phone can provide this information.

As a general rule, salmon and steelhead come in on the flood tide (incoming tide). On the ebb tide (outgoing), the forces of water between the downstream flow and the outgoing tide will be too strong for the fish to want to exert more energy than needed to move upriver. So, on the ebb tide you'll want to fish near the mouth of the river. Fish will tend to school-up at or near the mouth and stage themselves before they move up with the flood tide.

As the flood tide begins, fish slowly begin to move up. The stronger the tidal movement, the greater distance they will travel upstream. It's best to try and fish at a location between the incoming tide water and the down flow of the river, at the point of least resistance, as they will tend to hold in these areas. At slack tide, you should be able to find fish from the mouth up.

As the tide begins to swing to ebb, again, your best bet is to go upriver, out of the tide water. Why? Because fish out of the tidal flow will feel comfortable staying in that section of river before resting and moving upstream in a normal progression. Those that are caught in the tidal push will either return back to the mouth or tuck in someplace to get out of the stronger currents. They may be holding at this point, but more than likely won't be on the bite because they're already using too much energy to just hold position.

Hatcheries

With most rivers, one of the obvious areas to target salmon and steelhead is near the hatchery. Fish stage themselves below the hatchery and move up when appropriate. You'll also see the majority of fishermen here for this very reason. But fish are holding throughout the rivers and there will be several holding areas in each system. To get away from the crowds you may want to fish downstream a bit and follow the guidelines above to find your own holes. While there may not be the numbers of fish that there are generally in front of the hatcheries, the chances of getting fresher, hotter fish are greater.

To improve your odds there are a few things we can do to make sure we have the best chance to catch salmon and steelhead. The best advice I can give anyone is to target hatchery salmon and steelhead during the peak of the runs, and target them near the hatchery itself. The more fish that are in the river, the better chance you have of one of them being interested in your presentation.

Fishing the canyons is a whole new experience.

Here are some important tips to remember when targeting hatchery fish:

- Fish during the height of the run
- Fish near the hatchery
- Use techniques you are familiar with
- If using bait, use good bait
- Use light setups
- Run n Gun (cover water and move on)
- Be stealthy
- Network to get reliable information

Techniques are personal preference. Hatchery steelhead tend to go for a good drift presentation of eggs or shrimp. I'm partial to float-and-jig fishing and hatchery fish do love the pink/white combos (no bait). For salmon, good bait from a float or drift is hard to beat. From a boat it's hard to beat side drifting for steelhead or back bouncing for salmon. These techniques are all covered in Chapter 6: Fishing Methods.

Chapter 5
Reading Water

Reading water also helps with navigation.

The ability to read water can truly be a gift. If you can think like a fish and know where a fish is likely to hold or swim, then most of the hard work is done. Mentioned in the previous chapter are water types that both salmon and steelhead like to hold in, but finding that water is not always so cut and dried. Those holes as described are few and far between; no two holes are identical.

When approaching a new hole there are certain characteristics you need to look for that can make the difference between catching fish and casting practice.

Structure

First of all, look for structure. Remember, fish need to feel they have some security, and structure will provide that. Sometimes structure is not clearly visible and this is where reading water comes into play. Can you see from the surface to the bottom of the hole? If not, some interpretation needs to take place. Look for

swirls, a good indication something is breaking up the natural flow of the water below the surface. If it's a boulder, chances are a fish could be holding behind or alongside of it. If it's a snag, even more reason to attack it. You may lose some gear, but remember fish are looking for a safe haven, don't be afraid to fish where others don't. You'd be surprised at how often people pass up nasty water because they don't want to re-tie, when in fact they probably also passed up fish.

Once you find the structure, try to gauge the speed of the river, not only on the surface but below as well. The perfect speed is about the same as a brisk walk. This holds true for most species. Coho and chum, however, tend to hold in frog water and sloughs as previously discussed. Water that looks consistent all the way across the hole will more often than not have a slot where the flow is actually slightly faster. This would be the path of least resistance and also where you'll find the majority of the fish. How many times have we fished a new portion of a river and fished the wrong side? Those that have already fished the river will know where these slots are and consistently catch fish. Take mental notes as to where fish are hooked. Chances are these are holding spots and fish often hold in these same locations unless the bottom or flow of the river changes, which they often do.

One of the most important characteristics to look for is seams, where fast water meets slow water. It is on either side of the seam that a salmon or steelhead will hold depending on conditions. Under normal conditions, the fish will hold just on the edge of the seam closest to the bank. Even if you're fishing from the bank on the same side of the river as the seam, fish tight, that's where the fish are. During high water conditions, most fish tend to be on the slow side of the seam, which again will most likely be nearest the bank. Under low water conditions, fish will tend to be on the fast side of the seam if they need more oxygen, and again the path of least resistance comes into play here. Remember these are guidelines as the fish can be on either side of the seam, but if there is a seam, you'll want to fish it.

Visibility

Visibility is an important factor when fishing a river. Although salmon and steelhead have a great sense of smell, they still like to see what they're about to strike. The fish gravitate towards darker water as it offers them a sense of security. They'll also gravitate towards colored-up water as the water is rising. As the water becomes even more cloudy and silty though, they soon realize it's not easy to survive in this kind of water and will seek clearer water if possible. They almost always move to the shores as the water becomes increasingly hard to stay comfortable in. The water runoff and stream runoff will provide enough clean water to keep the gills working properly. Also because there is actually some visibility in this runoff section and fish can see what's coming at them, they have a tendency to be on the bite during the short period between clean runoff and colored-up flood conditions.

Low, clear water can be fantastic. It can also turn a bite off. Because the fish need to feel some security, you must go into stealth mode to fish under ultra-clear conditions. Smaller presentations are also a must so as not to spook a fish with something that doesn't look natural. How often have we heard anglers begging for rain? This usually occurs when the water is low and clear. Rain will help color-up the water a little, bring fresh fish in, get them on the move and get them on the bite.

Anything over 2 feet of visibility is great—4 to 6 feet optimal. With visibility in this range, all fishing techniques can be utilized effectively.

Water Temperature

Water temperature is an important factor, but for some reason most anglers don't even pay attention to it. Find the experts and it'll be hard to find one that doesn't.

Extremely cold water conditions—say under 40 degrees—are very tough to fish. The fish tend to be lethargic and not interested in biting at all. Water will usually fall into this category under long-term cold spells with no rain. The water becomes incredibly clear and the fish seek slower-moving water where they generally would not hold. I've found that under these conditions a properly presented jig moving through this slower water can draw strikes from both salmon and steelhead.

Normal winter water temperatures are usually in the 40- to 50-degree range. The closer to 50 degrees the more active the fish will be. An ideal situation can occur when the water has been

(Top) What's the water saying.
(Center) Summer conditions still produce steelhead.
(Bottom) Reading the water.

Hefty steelhead.

Cold water requires a slower presentation.

below 40 degrees and then a rainstorm moves in and floods the river. The rain and snow-melt will be warmer than the river and bring the temperature up. As the river begins to drop and clear up, the fishing should be dynamite! Well, that won't always happen when you want it to, but as long as the water temperature is in this normal range there should be fish to fish for.

Normal spring/summer water conditions are in the 50- to 60-degree range. Salmon and steelhead are very active in this temperature range, thus the term "hot" fish; not only active biters but active fighters as well. Water temperatures in this range combined with a little color in the river tend to be ingredients for outstanding fishing.

Extremely warm water temperatures—over 60 degrees—I wouldn't want to fish. Leave the holes for the swimmers and hope the fish survive. Not only will it be uncomfortable for the fish to

maneuver in temperatures above 60 degrees, but you can pretty much count on them being off the bite. Don't be a loogan!

I've mentioned the importance of the weather forecast. I'm mentioning it again in this section so you become accustomed to looking at the weather to be able to read the water. This doesn't mean looking at the water to determine what lies underneath. This means taking the forecast into consideration, to know what to expect from experience on the sections of rivers you've already seen under similar conditions.

This is a very brief description on reading water, when considering all that has been written on this subject, but follow these guidelines, along with all the other information in this book and you'll become a more successful fisherman.

Now let's get to fishing!

Chapter 6
Techniques

Big fish love big worms like this 6-inch orange worm from Mad River.

Everyone has their favorite fishing technique. Mine happens to be float-fishing. But the truth of the matter is if you rely solely on one technique you will be passing up a lot of opportunities to catch fish.

No single technique will be suitable for every section of river, nor will it be the best choice for every species of fish. The idea here is to know and be proficient in the use of multiple techniques so that given any set of conditions you might find yourself fishing you will be prepared to select and use the one or two techniques that are most likely to bring you success.

The techniques discussed below fall into one of three general categories, but they may also have things in common with the others. The general categories are: natural presentation, attraction and intimidation.

Natural presentation includes techniques such as float-fishing and drift fishing while attraction includes methods such as back-bouncing and plunking, although many of the items in this category cross over into the other two. Intimidation, for the most part, is made up of techniques using lures such as plugs, spinners and spoons.

A thorough knowledge of all the techniques discussed below, and knowing when and where to apply them, will both greatly enrich your time on the water and help you hook and land more fish. Now that's a win-win scenario if ever I've seen one!

Since many techniques incorporate the same lures or bait, I've summarized those below.

Drift Bobbers

Since their inception, probably more steelhead and salmon have been caught in rivers all over the world on drift bobbers than any other lure. When fished in rivers for salmon or steelhead drift bobbers can be fished alone, with a piece of yarn or with bait.

The idea of the drift bobber is to look like eggs as they float down the river. Being buoyant they lift your presentation off the bottom. How much will depend on river flow, whether or not you have bait along with the bobber, and leader length. The longer the leader, the higher the bobber will float. The slower the water, the higher too. Remember this when tying up, realizing you want the bobber to be in the strike zone, 1 to 2 feet off the bottom.

You'll want to utilize the smallest size drift bobber you can for normal to clear water conditions. In higher water you may even have to use two in tandem to get your presentation to float up high enough into the zone.

Hook size is relevant to the size of the bobber. The bobber should fit in-between the point and the shank of the hook. Too large a bobber will interfere with the bite.

The most popular drift bobbers are Lil' Corkies, Cheaters, Winners and the old Okie Drifter.

Winged Bobbers

This type of bobber uses the same principles as the drift bobber, except with wings. The wings cause the bobber to spin in the current, creating both noise and extra attraction. The use of a winged bobber is preferred when fishing very slow water where the turning will create action not provided by a drift bobber alone. Spin-N-Glos and Birdie Drifters are the most common winged bobbers. Smile blades react the same way winged bobbers do except they have no body, they're also a great way to create noise and attraction while maintaining a smaller profile.

Jigs

They look somewhat like a fly but they have a lead head. The head is usually painted and material such as marabou or rabbit fur is attached so when floating down the river the jig comes alive. Probably one of the most effective lures we fish today.

Beads

Glass or plastic beads simulate eggs like a drift bobber, except they are non-buoyant. They are used more as an add-on for other lures, but can be fished alone if the technique you're using keeps them off the bottom. Adding beads is most widely used as added attractant but can also be used for spaces or bumpers between knots and terminal gear.

Yarn

Nylon yarn or wool as it's referred to in Canada, might be the single most versatile lure of all. Yarn comes in many colors to complete your color scheme, from neutral egg colors, to shrimp, to fluorescent for those dark river days when you need that extra attractant. Not only does yarn act as an attractant but it also does two very important things that might help you in hooking more fish. One, it holds scent. Two, the fibers tend to get caught in a fish's mouth possibly giving you more time to set the hook should you be slow on the hook-set. Yarn also is the primary component of a yarnie, rag or Glo Bug. Are you a UV fan? The fluorescent pigment in the yarn is also UV.

Pink Worms

Well, they don't have to be pink, but pink is by far the most popular and productive color of all the worms out there. As the name implies they are worms. Most are buoyant or semi-buoyant therefore a shorter leader is commonly used so the worm doesn't float out of the strike zone. Although many worms are scented, some are not. If they are not scented it is recommended to add scent where legal so they don't smell like plastic. Pink worms can be fished alone or on a jig head.

Bait

Good cured roe (eggs) is hard to beat for salmon or steelhead and there are plenty of great cures out there right from the jar. For some of my preferred cure recipes see Appendix A.

PAUL ISHII

CHRIS SHAFFER

LUKE FILMER

(Top) An assortment of plugs.
(Center) Drift fishing gold.
(Bottom) If you want to keep your trophy fish get a replica made like this one from Blackwater Fish Replicas.

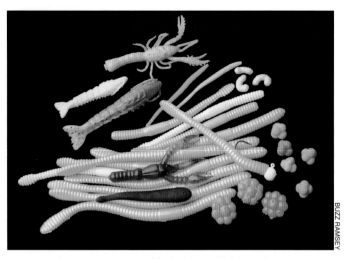

An assortment of baits from Yakima Bait.

Along with roe, sand shrimp, coon shrimp or prawns are right behind as effective bait. Night crawlers and squid are also effective for steelhead. A new bait technique that has been killer on spring chinook is tuna balls. Just your canned tuna in oil tied up in a mesh sack (roe sack) to the desired size. The dirtier the water the larger the ball, up to about the size of a golf ball.

Roe Sack

Mesh material can be used to gather any number of eggs from just a couple to a cluster, then wrapped with magic thread to form a sack. Very popular in the Great Lakes and Canada, these sacks keep the eggs in cluster form. Roe sacks should be changed when the eggs don't milk out anymore.

Imitation Bait

With technology comes progress, even when it comes to bait. There is a wide variety of imitation baits made from various materials and injected with scent that come amazingly close to the real thing. Although fresh bait is preferred, these imitations aren't a bad second choice and the benefit is they stay on your hook much longer. When using imitations I always add scent when legal to do so, as I don't think salmon or steelhead are fond of a plastic or rubber smell. Remember, even if they are fake, if they have scent injected they are considered bait on most waters, so make sure and check the regulations.

Float fishing from the boat.

Scent

If bait isn't available, or even if it is, the use of scent is important not only as an attractant but also to mask human scent. Experimenting with different scent until you find your go-to scent is common. My favorites are shrimp for steelhead, and shrimp/anise mix for salmon. Make sure and put scent on the lure, but a little on the line and weight won't hurt either. Read the regulations because in all the areas that I know, scent is considered bait. So if there is a no-bait restriction, this means no scent either.

Drift Fishing

Lure: Drift Bobbers, Wing Bobbers, Pink Worm, Yarn, Bait, Beads, Scent

Water: Slow to faster-moving water, trenches, slots and flats

Float-fishing, as I previously stated, is my favorite technique, but the most productive technique of all time for salmon and steelhead, and the technique I think all fishermen should start out learning, is drift fishing. Once you become comfortable with the aspects of drift fishing you will have a more thorough understanding of how fish bite and react to your presentation. You'll also have a feel for the bottom structure and how your presentation reacts—an important factor when reading water.

The idea of drift fishing is to let your presentation drift along the bottom in the strike zone in the most natural way. It's a simple statement but a difficult technique to perfect.

Standard Drift

I don't know if Bill Herzog coined the phrase "standard drift", but since I consider him a master at this technique and that's what he calls it, we'll go with it. It is very simple to rig a bobber for drift fishing, and the setup will be based on the river you are fishing, the type of fish you are after and how much water flow the river has. You'll want to use a quality monofilament main line of 8- to 12-pound test for steelhead, up to 25-pound test for chinook. The main line should be tied to a barrel swivel and at the other end of the swivel add a leader of 18 to 48 inches. The leader should also be of a quality monofilament or fluorocarbon and can be a lighter pound test than the main line. The drift bobber is strung on the leader ahead of the hook before the leader is tied to the barrel swivel. Leave a long tag end so you can attach hollow-core lead.

Alternate weight systems include using a 3-way swivel with one of the three being a snap swivel with a slinky attached to it. The old-school method would be to slide a piece of surgical tubing on the main-line and insert a piece of pencil lead into the tubing.

It's important that the rig drifts naturally as it moves downstream. The right-sized drift bobber will help do this. A bobber that is too big will float the hook and bait too high over the fish. A bobber that is too small will not float the hook and bait high enough, resulting in snags and hang-ups. The objective is to rig the correctly sized drift bobber to create a neutral-buoyancy situation, where it floats naturally, just up off the bottom of the river as it drifts. Leader length and size of drift bobber are normally determined by water condition, size of hook and size of bait. In water that is high and milky or off-colored, a shorter leader of 18 to 24 inches is all that is required, so you can get away with using a larger drift bobber and not have to worry about it floating out of the strike zone. In low, clear water, a longer leader of 32 to 48 inches coupled with a smaller drift bobber is recommended.

Good holding water for salmon or steelhead, also known as a drift, is water that is usually above or below some rapids or swift water. The fish like to hold in this water and rest before continuing their journey upstream. This holding water is generally 4 to 12 feet deep.

When casting, it is important that the presentation be "ticking" the bottom as it comes through the hole. In order to achieve this you must cast your presentation above the hole. The one thing you don't want to do is cast too far upstream which will cause undue snags. Position yourself on the river so that you are across from the hole (12 o'clock) and cast between 10 and 11 o'clock if the river is flowing to your right, or between 1 and 2 o'clock if it is flowing to your left. The combination of current speed and depth will determine the amount of weight you will need to use in order to get your presentation to drift properly through the strike zone.

As your presentation drifts through the hole you'll want to make sure not to "jerk" at every little movement. Each time you jerk it pulls it up and out of the zone and also causes unnatural movement. It does take time to recognize a strike but soon it will become second nature and you'll begin to rely on instinct.

Cover the entire hole, visualizing a grid as you cast. Try and slice the water up in two-foot sections, making sure your presentation passes over each 2-foot grid. As your line tightens up it will begin to swing in towards you. As long as you are maintaining contact with the bottom every few seconds you're fine. If your presentation begins to lift off the bottom, either reel in or feed it line. If you would like an extended drift in longer holes, feed some line before the line starts to swing in. Bait-casters are really the preferred reel here so you can keep the spool disengaged to allow line to feed out slowly and naturally, but if a fish strikes you can thumb it to set the hook before taking the time to engage the spool. If you let out line too fast your presentation will sit on the bottom, possibly becoming hung up.

I prefer to walk the hole down while drift fishing rather than extending the drift with the technique mentioned above. You'll find that many fish hit on that swinging motion of the standard drift. Also, if at the end of your swing you're still in holding water, let it sit for a few seconds before reeling in. Many times fish will follow your presentation as it swings in and that hesitation at the end may entice a strike; it's happened many times.

PHIL STEPHENS

Free-drifting proved lethal for a trio of steelhead.

Side Drifting

Think of drift fishing from a drift boat while the boat is moving. Kind of a weird thought but this is pretty much what side drifting is. The idea here is to cover a complete hole in one drift as it can be tough to achieve a second drift depending on water current and how fit the oarsman is. As you approach a hole with the drift boat, the oarsman must slow down and row against the current to slow down the speed of the drift. The idea is to move downstream at about half the speed of the current. Those fishing will cast straight across or ever so slightly downstream. As the boat is moving, this will allow the presentation to drop into the strike zone more rapidly, but because it's slower than the current speed if you cast upstream you pose a greater risk of hanging up or dragging.

As with all forms of drift fishing, you'll want your weight to tick the bottom every few feet. With side drifting, and with free drifting as discussed below, it doesn't need to be quite as frequent as from the bank. As long as there's a tick every 10 to 15 feet you'll be good.

As the presentation continues down the hole it will start to swing in, just as in bank fishing. At this time, reel in and re-cast. By continuing to do this you'll achieve a greater number of casts

★ Slow action for side drifting or free drifting	**Drift Fishing**					
Species	**Rod**	**Rating**	**Action★**	**Reel**	**Line**	**Leader**
Steelhead	8'6" to 9'6"	8 - 12lbs	Fast	2500 spin or 100 to 200 Baitcaster	Mono: 8-12lb	Mono: 6-12lb or Fluorocarbon 6-12lb
Coho	8'6" to 9'	8 - 15lbs	Fast	2500 Spin or 100 to 200 Baitcaster	Mono: 10-15lb	Mono: 10-15lb or Fluorocarbon 10-15lb
Chinook	9' to 10'	10 - 20lbs	Fast	200 to 300 Baitcaster	Mono: 15-25lb	Mono: 20lb
Chum	8'6" to 9'	10 - 20lbs	Fast	200 to 300 Baitcaster	Mono: 15-20lb	Mono: 15-20lb
Pinks	7'6" to 9'	6 - 12lbs	Fast	2500 Spin	Mono: 6-10lb	Mono: 6-10lb or Fluorocarbon 6-10lb

Mark Par used a roe sack to encourage this metalhead to bite.

throughout the hole being covered than by just drifting through and not slowing down the speed of the boat.

The standard side drifting rig is two #4 hooks with a drift bobber tied in between for steelhead, or two 1/0 to 2/0 hooks for salmon. In the bait loop of the top hook, place some salmon roe, shrimp or yarn. Hit it with some scent as well so if the bait falls off during the cast or an unnecessary jerk, the lure will still have scent.

A Yarnie with a single #2 hook for steelhead, or 2/0 to 3/0 for salmon is a great, underutilized alternative. Sometimes that nice fluffy presentation with some scent will outperform bait itself.

A very light and slow-action rod is best suited for this style of fishing. The "give" in the slow action helps set the hook and is more forgiving than the faster-action rods preferred from the bank.

Although the oarsman cannot fish using this method, all fish will be the result of how effective he/she is at putting you in the correct position and slowing enough to allow those fishing to cover all the water in the hole thoroughly.

Free Drifting

Also called boondoggin, free drifting is arguably the most productive method for steelhead fishing from a boat, and pretty dang effective for salmon as well. To properly free drift, a sled is required. One could argue that you could free drift from a

drift boat, but there wouldn't be much reason for doing so. The main idea behind this technique is to cover a long hole while naturally presenting the bait at the current speed. To do this from a sled, the boat is positioned above the hole and within comfortable casting distance from the hole itself, running parallel to the bank.

Once the boat is across from the hole, those fishing will cast upstream at an approximately 45-degree angle. The person in the bow of the boat should cast first, followed in order by those in the back. It's the person driving the boat who is responsible for maintaining the current speed while staying parallel to the bank; not always an easy task while moving down river with the current. Positioning is crucial here and when positioned properly, this method is deadly. You'll want your presentation to tick the bottom every 3-5 seconds to maintain your position in the strike zone. If the boat travels too slowly, your presentation will begin to run across from the boat or downstream—you do not want this to occur. The boat needs to allow the current to dictate the speed, while the person in charge of the boat just makes sure the boat is parallel to the bank. If the presentation begins to come equal with the boat, reel up and re-cast upstream trying to hold a position of approximately 10-11 o'clock moving to the right, or 1-2 o'clock moving to the left.

The same setups used for side drifting are utilized for free drifting as well. Done properly, free drifting will put fish to the boat.

Species Specific

Steelhead

Drift fishing has accounted for more steelhead than all other methods combined. Most often when talking about steelhead fishing, drift fishing is pretty much assumed. As float-fishing becomes more popular it may not be the case one day, but that time has not yet come. A properly presented corkie, yarn and egg combo is pretty much unbeatable when it comes to hooking steelhead; the offering just can't be passed up. From the bank you should always plan on having a drift rod setup with you as you can fish so many different holes this way. From a drift boat, side drifting is just plain deadly. From a sled, free drifting is plain nuts. You simply cannot match the numbers with any other technique for steelhead as you can with these two.

Coho

Use a slightly larger sized presentation than what is used for steelhead with eggs or shrimp and you have a setup that can attract coho and/or steelhead. Not the most effective method for coho, but when both species are present there is a chance at either of them.

Chinook

Not my favorite method for chinook, but it will work. There are much more productive methods; float-fishing, plugs and back-bouncing to name a few.

Chum & Pinks

Occasionally you'll hook up with these species, but they don't often bite this way. More often than not they'll be flossed or lined (this happens when the leader or line runs into the fish's mouth as it swims. The angler feeling the tension, pulls the rod, which in turn pulls the hook into the outside of the mouth).

Float-Fishing: All Species

Lure: Jigs, Bait
Water: Slow

Float-fishing is extremely effective. It's been called many things from bobber fishing to sissy fishing; the latter by those

Float setup.

that don't understand the complexities of the technique and think it's only for beginners. Many of those that haven't tried it will be converted once they realize the effectiveness of a natural presentation, and float-fishing provides the most natural of all the techniques when performed correctly. In the 1990's I was one of the few who called float-fishing my go-to technique and many times I would be fishing alongside others who wouldn't give it a try. It doesn't take long to catch on when you hook a few fish while everyone else is getting skunked. Now this doesn't happen on all water, but given the right circumstances and a hole made for float-fishing, other techniques just don't match up. Float-fishing has become very popular as others have seen just how effective this technique is.

The idea is to present your lure or bait through the holding water with the most natural appearance possible. When drift fishing you want to tick the bottom to know you're in the strike zone. When it comes to float-fishing, those ticks are a no-no. Each time it ticks the bottom it stops the natural appearance and means your presentation is on the bottom. Ideally, you want your lure or bait to be within 1 or 2 feet of the bottom. Whether you're using a fixed float or sliding float, make sure the length is adjustable because you'll be varying the length throughout the day. Normally

Float Fishing

* This does not include center-pin rods/reels

Species	Rod★	Rating	Action	Reel	Line	Leader
Steelhead	9' to 10'6"	6 - 12lbs	Moderate	2500 spin or 100 to 200 Baitcaster	Braid: 20-30lb	Fluorocarbon 6-12lb
Coho	9' to 10'6"	10 - 15lbs	Moderate	2500 Spin or 100 to 200 Baitcaster	Braid: 20-30lb	Mono: 10-15lb or Fluorocarbon 10-15lb
Chinook	9' to 10'6"	10 - 20lbs	Moderate	200 to 300 Baitcaster	Braid: 20-30lb	Mono: 20-30lb or Fluorocarbon 20-30lb
Chum	9' to 10'6"	10 - 20lbs	Moderate	200 to 300 Baitcaster	Braid: 20-30lb	Mono: 15-20lb
Pinks	9' to 10'6"	6 - 12lbs	Moderate	2500 Spin	Braid: 20-30lb	Fluorocarbon 6-10lb
Sockeye	9' to 10'6"	6 - 12lbs	Moderate	2500 Spin	Braid: 20-30lb	Fluorocarbon 6-10lb

GIL MCKEAN

DANIEL BRAVO

MIKE ZAVADLOV

MIKE ZAVADLOV

(Top left) Spinners work great for chinook.
(Bottom left) Twitchin jigs is ultra effective for coho.
(Top right) The pink worm has proven effective over and over.
(Top center) Bill Herzog with a trophy coho.
(Bottom right) Jigs, I love 'em.

Float coming at ya!

you'll cast above the hole so your presentation has time to sink down and start a natural flow before it gets to the hole. Looking at the float, your presentation will be correct if the float is perfectly straight up and down.

As your presentation moves downstream, if the top of the float is angled more downstream this is an indication that it's hitting bottom; reel up and adjust the float so there is less length to your lure. If you cast again and the same thing happens, continue adjusting until your float runs perpendicular to the water. If you're dragging, you're not fishing.

If you're too high in the water column you can still catch fish but not as effectively as being within 1 or 2 feet of the bottom. To make sure you're in that zone it's always better to find bottom on the first few casts and adjust the length shorter, rather than starting out too short and not knowing how far off the bottom you are.

If the float happens to be angled upstream when traveling downstream, this would be an indication that you're either holding back the float due to line drag, your line is not coming off the reel smoothly enough, or the lure is moving faster than the float. The first scenario is easy, feed it more line and make sure it's a drag-free float. If your line is free-spooling and the float is still angled upstream, add some more weight, usually a split shot or two will do the trick. Again, to be float-fishing effectively, make sure the float runs perpendicular to the water's surface.

Make sure your float and lure are properly balanced. You'll notice on most floats there are three colors. The main body, usually black, neutral or clear, followed by a thin line which is the water indicator, then the top color which is the sight indicator. To be properly balanced the water level should be near the water indicator line. It doesn't have to be exact, but should be close. One way to ensure proper balance is to match known weights of lures, weight and floats before casting.

Lure weight should equal float weight (example: 1/8-ounce jig, use a 1/8-ounce float). Many times you'll need more than just the lure or bait, so the use of weight is desired—it not only makes it easier to cast but also gets the lure down into the strike zone quicker and holds it there. In this case, lure weight + weight = float size (1/8-ounce jig + 1/4-ounce weight = 3/8-ounce float).

When adding bait you don't need to increase the float size as bait is semi buoyant. You'll want to have something weighing down the bait, be it a jig, lead or split shots. Match up the float size with the weight used (egg cluster plus 1/2-ounce pencil lead = 1/2-ounce float). You only want an 18-24" leader when fishing bait alone as it will float higher than the lead.

Now that you have your perfectly balanced float and are in the strike zone, hold on! When the float goes down, set the hook. Ah, that's too easy right? Yes, those are very common strikes and the easiest to detect. But, how many strikes are you missing? What happens if the float pops up? Well, that's a fish. Remember your presentation is pulling the float down to the water indicator line. If a fish grabs your lure but continues up the water column instead of back down, it removes the pressure that is holding the float down so it pops up—set the hook. What about if your float starts twitching? If you're fishing for chinook it generally means a fish has your presentation and is mouthing it, something chinook are known for—again, set the hook. Basically, any variation in the natural drift of the float indicates either a fish, the bottom, or a fish. Two out of three times are good enough odds that you should

Chris Shaffer is all smiles.

set the hook when your float reacts any way other than natural.

To keep your float natural throughout the hole, you need a drag-free drift. The longer the drift the harder it will be to keep your line off the water. This is not always possible. When it does lie on the water, braided line is handy as it has a natural ability to float rather than sink. The more line that's on the water, the more the current will grab the line and move it downstream quicker than the float itself. We need to mend the line at this time. When there is line downstream of the float it will pull on the float and cause it not to be perpendicular anymore. To mend it you'll want to point your rod at the line and with one gentle motion lift the rod and line off the water and place it upstream of the float. You don't want too much slack but as long as the line is upstream from the float it will run true. Depending on how far you cast, how long the drift is and the water current, you may need to mend your line several times for each drift, although sometimes you won't at all.

With float-fishing you can cover so much water it's almost unfair. I slice the water into 2-foot sections, making sure my presentation follows the hole through each of these slices. I like to work from one side of the hole to the other, hoping if a fish doesn't like my lure the first time it will move away until there's no more room to move, thus irritating the fish enough to cause it to strike out of fear. Of course, I'm hopeful the fish will love my presentation and travel several feet out of its holding area to attack my offering with a vengeance.

Species Specific

Steelhead

Jigs are the perfect lure for float-fishing for steelhead. I'm not sure what the fish think they are, but a jig will often out-fish bait if presented correctly. 1/8-ounce marabou jigs are the most popular and what I fish 90 percent of the time when float-fishing for steelhead. I do not add bait or scent to a jig when fishing for steelhead, you don't need to. I have several friends that are great fishermen that do add bait, mostly prawn meat, to a jig and are very successful. The addition of a small pink worm (3-4 inches) to a jig head can be extremely effective and I fish these often. Those with a paddle tail work best.

Chum

Jigs with either prawn or shrimp can be deadly when fishing for chum. Bright colors of pink, purple, cerise or chartreuse are best

used in all water types, even clear. Once again, the addition of a pink worm is also extremely effective on a jig head.

Pinks

Pinks love pink! Anything you can float that is pink will be effective for catching these feisty little fish, but a 1/8-ounce pink jig or a pink worm on a jig head work best. Even a small flutter spoon, like a Dick Nite under a float, works but the addition of weight is needed to keep the spoon in the zone.

Sockeye

Want to catch sockeye? By far the most effective method for catching sockeye legally in the rivers is via float and jig, with a piece of prawn. In Alaska they have a technique called the Kenai flop, which is a glorified way of legally flossing. In all other rivers in the world sockeye go nuts for a well-presented jig with prawn presentation.

Coho

Coho are probably the species least fished with a float. Will they bite? Yes, but generally not that often. Coho prefer a more active presentation so if you do float a jig, give it a little twitch once in a while using a marabou jig with a long tail. I'd look at twitchin', spinners or spoons when targeting this species.

Chinook

Chinook aren't great candidates for a jig and float, even with bait. Float a nice cluster of eggs by them though and it can be lights out. Chinook are especially susceptible to a slow-milking egg cluster traveling through the strike zone under a float. This has been the go-to method for those seeking chinook on most rivers. The addition of a sand shrimp, or sand shrimp tail, to the egg cluster (AKA shrimp cocktail) will sometimes kick in the bite when eggs alone won't do.

Twitchin'

Lure: Jigs, Hootchies
Water: Slow to non-moving deep holes, sloughs

Twitchin' is a rather new technique that has become very popular, especially when targeting coho, pinks, sockeye or chum. The use of a jig when "twitched" with the correct motion can turn on a bite more than any other technique if the fish seem to be lock-jawed. This is also one of the most exciting techniques because when a salmon attacks your lure they're not shy about it and will try to rip the rod from your hands.

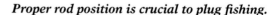
Proper rod position is crucial to plug fishing.

Once you have the rod and reel selected, choose a jig with the proper color and weight to match the conditions. See below for species specific technique.

Tie a 1/4-ounce to 5/8-ounce twitchin' jig directly to the main line. A twitchin' jig is simply the same style jig used for float-fishing except it will have longer material, or tail, and have a slightly larger hook. If using braid, tie a Palomar knot, if mono, a UNI or improved clinch knot will work nicely.

Cast your jig and let it settle down towards the bottom. Engage the reel, and then set your first twitch. It's all in the wrist! Assuming your jig is at the 12 o'clock position, I've found the best way to hold your rod is across your body with the rod tip pointed at approximately 11 o'clock (or 1 o'clock if you're left handed). Then, using your wrist only, twitch the rod towards your body so the tip only moves 1 to 1 1/2 feet. Because the motion is moving the jig towards you as you twitch, it should only raise the jig 6-10 inches with the rest of the movement being horizontal in the current.

When first getting started you'll notice this isn't much movement at the point of the wrist, but this is the most effective motion. The longer the rod, the less wrist action required but it is also more difficult. After the initial movement, return the rod back to 11 o'clock while reeling in the slack. This is also very slight, most often only half or three-quarters of a handle crank.

You don't want to crank too much or too fast as this will pull the jig up too far off the bottom and out of the strike zone. It's possible that you won't have to crank on every twitch; all this will vary according to river flow, jig size and amount of the actual twitch. Make sure the jig maintains its position within the bottom two feet of the river to be effectively in the strike zone during the twitchin' process.

On holes that have some current, you may not have to reel at all if the pressure from the flow keeps the jig moving downstream and removes the slack on the downward motion. Once you get the motion down, you'll realize it's a very fluid and continuous twitch-and-reel, or in the latter case just twitch and wait until the slack is out, then twitch again. Fish will most often hit the jig on the fall, so the next twitch will often stick the hook enough to give you ample time to set it. With a sensitive rod you can actually feel missed hits, but continue to twitch and they will just annihilate it.

There's nothing boring about this technique, that's for sure. You feel everything and the thrill of this form of fishing is unmatched. It takes a while to get the rhythm down, but once you do, it will soon become one of your favorite methods, as it has for me.

Species Specific

Pinks

Twitchin' for pinks is indisputably the best method for catching these smaller but very active fish. As with any method for pinks, use pink as the main color; 1/4-ounce jigs with pink marabou or rabbit's fur will work wonders for these feisty little fish. You'll find pinks in slow water, but tidal water is where you're going to want to target pinks for fresh fish. Twitchin' will work from a boat and from the bank.

Coho

Probably the most frustrating of the salmon species to catch, coho become lock-jawed quite often. Twitchin' jigs is one way of getting them interested in your lure. The jerking motion of a jig seems to drive these fish crazy and they can't seem to resist a well-presented lure. Darker colors in black and purple work best in normal to clear water, with bright pink used for more colored-up water. You'll find coho in the sloughs and slow water, but also in the deeper holes with a little current. Look for wood structure and cast your jig at the wood; that first twitch is an important one and often will draw a strike immediately. 1/4- to 3/8-ounce jigs are most common for coho. One type of jig that is deadly on coho can be quickly made by simply pulling a small hootchie in the colors mentioned above over a jig head.

Chum

Very aggressive biters and fierce fighters, twitchin' has become a great method to entice these big dogs. Larger jigs in 3/8 to 5/8 ounce, in bright pinks, purples and chartreuse are the favorite targets of these fish and when they hit you'll know it. Slower water and sloughs are where they'll be found.

Chinook

Although not an extremely effective method for chinook, they will attack a twitched jig. One of my most memorable chinook strikes

Twitchin'

Species	Rod	Rating	Action	Reel	Line	Leader
Coho	7'6" to 9'	8 - 15lbs	Fast	2500 Spin	Braid: 20 - 30lb	N/A: Direct Tie
Chinook	9' to 10'6"	10 - 20lbs	Fast	2500 Spin	Braid: 20 - 30lb	N/A: Direct Tie
Chum	8'6" to 10'6"	10 - 17lbs	Fast	2500 Spin	Braid: 20 - 30lb	N/A: Direct Tie
Pinks	7'6" to 8'6"	4 - 10lbs	Fast	2500 Spin	Braid: 20 - 30lb, or Mono: 10	N/A: Direct Tie
Sockeye	7'6" to 8'6"	4 - 10lbs	Fast	2500 Spin	Braid: 20 - 30lb, or Mono: 10	N/A: Direct Tie

Big coho are often enticed by a twitched jig.

came when I was looking at my jig about 1 foot below the surface next to the drift boat in order to see what the fish was seeing when suddenly a 24-pound chinook came up and engulfed the jig, almost yanking the rod from my hand. I learned several things from that strike—mainly, fish all the way to the boat. A chinook likes a more slowly presented twitch than other species do and, above all, hold on tight!

Steelhead

Twitchin' for steelhead is starting to pick up and more people are beginning to hook them using this method. I personally don't find it effective enough to pass up another method to try this technique, however, if you want to twitch a jig for steelhead, go for it!

Spinners

Species: All
Lure: Spinners
Water: Slow to non-moving deep holes, sloughs

One of the more exciting techniques, it's important to have a very sensitive rod so you're able to feel every turn of the blade. Blade speed is crucial, along with being in the strike zone. When casting a spinner we often need to hit the far end of a hole, or the bank, so we can cover lots of holding water. When the spinner first hits the water, let it sink. Once it's at or near the bottom, give it a quick twitch to set the blade in motion. You'll want to retrieve via your spinning reel as slowly as possible while still maintaining the blade's rotation. If the blade is not rotating, it's not fishing. If the blade is rotating too fast, you're not fishing effectively. Again, the slowest possible rotation of the blade is best.

It's also important to stay within the strike zone near the bottom of the hole. Retrieving too quickly will cause the spinner to rise. Current along with the retrieval may also bring the spinner up. An effective way to keep the spinner down, even against the current, is simply to lower your rod to the water. The less line angle, the lower in the water column the spinner will remain. You don't want a slack line as it will cause the blade to stop rotating. To start the rotation back up, a simple twitch will do the trick. If the blade will rotate on its own in the current, then don't reel in until the lure has finished the drift. Once the drift has finished, retrieve your spinner slowly to the boat or bank. Often fish follow the presentation right up to the angler and then strike. The spinner doesn't stop fishing until the blade stops moving.

Hook type is an important factor when spinner-fishing. Most come with treble hooks, but you're going to want to replace them with a high-quality siwash hook. The siwash will not only hook and hold the fish better, but will not hook up on the bottom as often as a treble will. The use of a siwash hook also enables a much easier release.

There are many spinners on the market. It's important to make sure that along with being balanced correctly, the spinner also produces noise. Noise is a great attractant. The rotating blade creates some noise, but the most effective spinners are created to make additional noise as well. Make sure you have some Vibrax, Vibrex or Panther Martin spinners in your bag as they are well-tested catching lures.

Spinner colors are also an important factor. For clear water black can be vital! "Black is back," and salmon and steelhead will hammer a black spinner or one with some black on it. In clear water I take some of my metal blades of antique brass or copper and color half of the blade black on each side with a Sharpie pen. Think of a 50/50 blade; half copper/antique brass, the other half black. Using brass or copper alone is also effective in clear water. Nickel can be effective as well, but I almost always add black because, for me, a nickel finish gives off too much reflection. Nickel also appears black to the fish below about 2 feet so in clear water this is fine, but in colored-up water you'll want to change it up.

In good colored water with visibility in the 4- to 10-foot range, the use of colors comes into play. I like less metal showing and more painted surfaces to attract the fish. Greens, blues and black are effective for salmon and steelhead. Reds, oranges, yellows and fluorescents I tend to save just for salmon.

With heavily colored-up water go back to metal because you need that flash to attract the fish. Gold, silver and brass all work well. The addition of fluorescent colors will add to the attraction, again moving towards more color for salmon, more metal for steelhead.

Coho love spinners

Species Specific

Steelhead

When fishing spinners for steelhead make sure the conditions are such that they will be active, meaning warmer, clear water in the winter, or most spring and summer runs. Tossing spinners into undercuts and getting the blade spinning quickly started can sometimes draw an aggressive strike from a steelhead that feels threatened from the sudden flash in its view.

Coho

Throwing spinners is a great way to fish for coho, in my mind only second to twitching for effectiveness. Find the wood and chuck the metal. Get right in with the branches, root wads and trees, and a slow blade rotating around the spinner can be irresistible to these fish. Bright fluorescent colors in all water conditions are best for coho, especially pink, orange and chartreuse. Attaching a small hootchie skirt to a spinner can turn the bite on during a lock-jaw period. Pink is always a great choice but black or purple are my favorites.

Chinook

Not my favorite technique for chinook, but if bait is not allowed I won't hesitate to throw a larger size 5 or 6 spinner to tempt them with. Keep it deep and slow, as with the other species, making sure you feel that slow thump of the blade. I like black and darker colors for chinook. A dark green body with a black blade has been my go-to color for chinook for a long time and has proven itself over and over.

In-line spinners are different. Mostly used in estuary fishing, in-line spinners have their place in larger rivers where you can troll downstream. Sounds kind of funky but that's because not too many rivers allow you to do this. We consistently hammer the fish with this technique on the Nushagak River in Alaska. Using a #7 blade in-line spinner with a 1- to 2-ounce dropper sinker, we troll

Spinners

Species	Rod	Rating	Action	Reel	Line	Leader
Steelhead	8'6" to 9'6"	8 - 15lbs	Fast	2500 spin or 100 to 200 Baitcaster	Braid: 20 - 30lb, or Mono: 10-15lb	N/A: Direct Tie
Coho	8'6" to 9'6"	8 - 15lbs	Fast	2500 Spin or 100 to 200 Baitcaster	Braid: 20 - 30lb	N/A: Direct Tie
Chinook	9' to 10'6"	10 - 20lbs	Fast	2500 Spin or 100 to 200 Baitcaster	Braid: 20 - 30lb	N/A: Direct Tie
Chum	8'6" to 9'6"	10 - 17lbs	Fast	2500 Spin or 100 to 200 Baitcaster	Braid: 20 - 30lb	N/A: Direct Tie
Pinks	7'6" to 9'	4 - 10lbs	Fast	2500 Spin or 100 to 200 Baitcaster	Braid: 20 - 30lb, or Mono: 10-15lb	N/A: Direct Tie

downstream fast enough to feel the blade thumping. The addition of a roe sack is a major plus when bait is allowed, and it will not throw off the balance because of the size of the spinner and the amount of flow that goes across the blade to keep it moving.

Chum

Fishing the same technique you use for coho will entice chum as well. Those bright colors on a slow-moving spinner are hard to pass up for these hard-fighting fish. Pink is especially effective.

Pinks

As with most techniques for pinks, just make sure it's pink! Small spinners in slow water are the ticket here.

Spoons

Species: All
Lure: 1/4-ounce to 1-ounce spoons
Water: Moderate to fast-moving water, typical drift fishing water works great.

When I was younger I refused to use spoons, not because they weren't effective but because most of the time when I saw a spoon and a fish together the spoon was stuck to its dorsal fin or tail. The spoon has been a long-time favorite of snaggers everywhere and I didn't want any part of that. But realizing that spoons can be effective when fished properly, I modified my thinking a little and have had some rather successful days "chucking metal". The first thing you should do is remove the treble hook and replace it with a high-quality, razor-sharp sickle hook.

Spoons are another technique which falls into the "chucking metal" category. A piece of metal tied directly onto your mainline has accounted for many fish since the inception of sport fishing. There is something about that flash the fish can't resist. Actually, the flash, wobble and movement of a spoon look like a small baitfish.

Cast out like you would a spinner, aiming directly across from you. Let it sink so it's near the bottom before engaging the reel or putting pressure on the reel with your thumb. Once engaged, or the line tightens due to pressure, the spoon will begin to flow with the current through the hole. The speed at which the spoon sinks depends on the width and thickness of the metal itself. Thinner blades sink faster and are more appropriate for deeper, faster water. Wider blades fish slow, shallow water better as water flowing across the body of the spoon helps keep it suspended instead of just quickly hitting the bottom. To properly fish the spoon it must wobble without turning over. If the spoon spins or turns over, then the retrieve is too fast or the amount of water running across the spoon is too great. This can also happen when holding back the spoon when your line tightens and the spoon begins to swing in. The natural temptation is to reel during the swing but you'll actually want to spool out some line so it maintains its position just above the bottom while still wobbling and covering water. Nothing wrong with it ticking the bottom a few times, in fact, this is a good thing, as long as it's not dragging.

The results of a battle with a "big boy."

A rock garden ready to be attacked.

JIM KUICH

Species Specific

Steelhead

Big steelhead love metal! A properly presented spoon has accounted for many trophy steelhead. Spoons may not be the most effective method for putting up numbers of steel, but the fish they hook are usually of the bigger variety. If you're after a trophy, start pitchin' 'em. Those older tarnished spoons are the ones I look for in most water. I also use a black or a blue Sharpie to dull the shine and create a different look. In off-colored water I'll leave full metal, but either gold or brass, nothing too shiny.

Coho

Spoons can be killer for coho as well. Again, not always the most effective method but you'll get some trophy-size fish and some rod-rippin' strikes. When pitchin' metal up tight against wood, coho often hit as the spoon is fluttering down to the bottom. Fish these spoons the same way you would for steelhead.

#1 Dick Nite Spoons in 50/50 or frog pattern work extremely well for coho in very slow water. When drift fishing with light lead and a 4-foot leader, coho have been known to stalk and attack these small spoons when nothing else will work. Consider them a stand-by lure after twitchin', spinners and regular spoons. The important thing to remember when fishing any spoon is to not let them turn over.

Pinks

Of course when fishing for pinks they'll hit anything colored in their namesake. All spoons will work given that they're pink, but a size 0 or "wee" Dick Nite in 50/50, frog or any color variation that includes the color pink is very effective. Drift fishing a Dick Nite is good, but I like to float-fish a Dick Nite in very slow water. For this method I'll take a 4-foot section of leader from my float to an in-line weight, then from the weight another 4-foot section of leader to the Dick Nite Spoon. Cast out and retrieve ultra-slowly so the spoon barely flutters. You'll know when one strikes—and they will.

Spoons

Species	Rod	Rating	Action	Reel	Line	Leader
Steelhead	8'6" to 9'6"	8 - 15lbs	Fast	2500 spin or 100 to 200 Baitcaster	Braid: 20 - 30lb, or Mono: 10-15lb	N/A: Direct Tie
Coho	8'6" to 9'6"	8 - 15lbs	Fast	2500 Spin or 100 to 200 Baitcaster	Braid: 20 - 30lb	N/A: Direct Tie
Chinook	9' to 10'6"	10 - 20lbs	Fast	2500 Spin or 100 to 200 Baitcaster	Braid: 20 - 30lb	N/A: Direct Tie
Chum	8'6" to 9'6"	10 - 17lbs	Fast	2500 Spin or 100 to 200 Baitcaster	Braid: 20 - 30lb	N/A: Direct Tie
Pinks	7'6" to 9'	4 - 10lbs	Fast	2500 Spin or 100 to 200 Baitcaster	Braid: 20 - 30lb, or Mono: 10-15lb	N/A: Direct Tie

(Top) Dr. Death.
(Center) Plunking lets you kick back and enjoy mother nature.
(Bottom) Eli Rico with a Mag Lip 3.5.

Plugs

Species: Steelhead, Chinook, Chum
Lure: Plugs
Water: Slow to moderate, mid to deep holes

Pulling plugs has been a regular part of salmon and steelhead fishing ever since fishermen in boats have learned to navigate the waters. Plugs are not as popular as they used to be, probably because many feel it's more boring than other methods, but produce they do, and generally bigger fish at that.

I was one of those fishermen who thought this method was boring so I would always pass in favor of another. Then I was fishing with Rob Endsley on the Skagit River one day and he asked if I wanted to fish plugs.

"Ah, no."

"Do you want to catch fish?" asked Rob.

"Well, yeah."

He handed me a plug rod and had me run the plug back 65 feet. I put that rod in the rod holder then picked up the other rod and ran it back the same distance and placed it in a rod holder as well.

Almost as if he pushed a button for the fish to hit he said, "OK, we're almost on them."

Then wham! Fish on.

Not two seconds later and damned if the other rod didn't go off as well.

Now I have a fish on and Rob's rod is going off too. Two fish on and Rob is cracking up. Not only cracking up, he can't grab his rod because he's rowing to shore. I can't grab it to give to him because my fish is going nuts and tail-walking across the river.

We ended up losing the second one but I managed to bring the first one to shore, a beautiful 14-pound hen, which was released.

"So plug fishing is boring, huh?" said Rob.

OK, point taken.

Before fishing a plug make sure it runs true. Whether it be for salmon or steelhead, a plug that runs erratically, lays over on its side while running, or does "loop-d-loops" in the water isn't going to do you many favors on the river. A well-tuned plug will dive deeper and subsequently hold in the fish's strike zone much longer than one that isn't tuned. To determine if a plug needs to be tuned, strip out some line and pull the plug alongside the boat against the current. I usually start by pulling gently on the first pass, a little harder on the second pass, and then I'll pull really hard on the final pass to make sure the plug will dive in strong current.

To begin the tuning process, check the belly and tail-screw eyes to ensure that they're straight. The eyes that the hooks are attached to act as rudders and if they aren't positioned properly no amount of tuning on the front eye will get the plug to run the way you want it to.

The final and most important step is to adjust the front eye on the bill of the plug, which accounts for the majority of the plug's action. Plugs like the Hot Shot come with an eye that's screwed into the plastic body of the plug and tuning consists of using pliers to twist the eye to the right or left until it runs straight. Twist the eye in the opposite direction the plug is diving, making minor adjustments until the plug passes the boatside test.

Plugs like the Wiggle Wart, Tadpolly, Flatfish and Brad's Wiggler, have an eye that's built directly into the plug. While these plugs may seem impossible to tune, using slight pressure with needle nose pliers to push the eye to the right or left can get these plugs running straight again. Like the front eye, the hook eyes on

A well-tuned plug can draw vicious strikes from big fish.

these plugs are also integrated right into the plug and if they're out of alignment they'll cause the plug to run to one side or the other. Be sure to check these in addition to the front eye.

Keeping the rods at a relatively low rod angle combined with the extra fast action of the rod, gives the plugs the cushion they need to keep working effectively. The use of rod holders is imperative to a high success rate. Wait until the rod buries itself and line starts coming off the reel, then set the hook.

Level-wind reels are a must for plug-fishing. All plugs must be the same distance behind the boat to create a "wall of death".

If the plugs are staggered the fish may swim between them, but if they're all at the same distance they can back a fish downstream and antagonize it into striking. A line counter makes this easy, but if line counters are not used count the number of passes of the line guide so that all rods are let out equally.

Scents are a given with plugs, unless there is a bait restriction. Even better than scent is "bait wrapping". Bait wrapping large plugs like Kwikfish and Flatfish serves not only to get a salmon or steelhead to hold onto the plug longer, it also masks the fisherman's scent.

Plugs

Species	Rod	Rating	Action	Reel	Line	Leader
Steelhead	7'6" to 8'6"	8 - 15lbs	Extra Fast	200 Baitcaster	Braid: 30 - 50lb	N/A: Direct Tie
Coho	7'6" to 8'6"	8 - 15lbs	Extra Fast	200 to 300 Baitcaster	Braid: 20 - 50lb	N/A: Direct Tie
Chinook	7'6" to 8'6"	10 - 20lbs	Extra Fast	300 Baitcaster	Braid: 20 - 65lb	N/A: Direct Tie
Chum	7'6" to 8'6"	10 - 17lbs	Extra Fast	200 to 300 Baitcaster	Braid: 20 - 50lb	N/A: Direct Tie

Negotiating the falls.

A sardine-wrapped plug produced this fish of a lifetime.

Of course, the perfect plug presented to an aggressive fish will usually draw a strike, but working a group of plugs together to draw strikes from both aggressive and somewhat passive fish is just one small piece of becoming a successful plug-fisherman. Depending upon water conditions, plug distance from the boat can vary between 35 and as much as 100 feet. Water visibility, flow and depth all play a role in determining the right distance. On average my steelhead plugs end up 50 to 60 feet from the boat under optimum conditions, and further as the waters get low and clear. Salmon plugging distances are much the same, though I'll tend to keep a little more distance between the boat and plugs when using the kicker motor to back troll.

Species Specific

Steelhead
Long, slot-type holes are best to plug fish for steelhead. Either the fish will attack immediately or they'll back down. By keeping a plug in their face and slowly working them back, many steelhead will bite out of frustration. Blues and greens work very well for steelhead. Hotshots, Tadpollies and River Rockers are fantastic steelhead plugs. When it comes to deeper slots the new Mag Lip 3.5 is amazing.

Chinook
Big plugs, big fish. Mag Lips, Flatfish and Kwikfish are the tickets here. These beasts can't resist a well-tuned plug. Sardine wrapped plugs will increase your catch rates. Silver, chartreuse, orange and cerise are some of the more productive colors.

Chum
Same method as for chinook, these are meat eaters with a ferocious appetite. Chum hold in water a little slower than chinook prefer, but you may also find them in the same holes. Chartreuse and purple are my go-to colors.

Divers

Lure: Bait
Water: Slow to moderately fast, mid to deep holes

There's no questioning the effectiveness of diver-and-bait presentations for both steelhead and salmon. Divers allow a slow, thorough presentation of bait to fish, with ample opportunity for even lethargic steelhead and salmon to develop an appetite. Successful diver fishing throughout the year means understanding the useful range of available products and the basics of rigging.

For the most part there are two general choices in divers. First is the crankbait type, including the Brad's Diver and the Mud Bug. The second choice is Luhr Jensen's Jet Divers, including models that achieve a maximum depth of 10, 20, 30, and 40 feet.

The proper diver choice does a few things. First, it gets your bait or lure to the bottom. Second, it handles the size of the bait or lure. And last, the right diver offers a smooth presentation from top to bottom of the run without constantly digging bottom. A diver that plows the bottom will put a move-stop, move-stop motion on the bait that's undesirable.

Bait diver.

The most effective baits to back-troll are coon shrimp, sand shrimp, prawns or eggs.

Because both salmon and steelhead will swallow a good presentation, I would encourage not using divers and bait when native fish are in the waters.

Just like plug-fishing, wait until the fish commits before setting the hook. This method is best fished with a rod holder to prevent premature hook-sets.

Species Specific

Steelhead
Fishing the same type of slots where you would a plug, back-trolling a diver and coon shrimp has become ultra-effective. Sand shrimp, prawns and eggs are not far behind.

Chinook
A shrimp cocktail with sand shrimp and eggs is pretty hard to beat for chinook. Keep the bait fresh and milking.

Back-Bouncing

Lure: Bait
Water: Moderate to moderate fast, mid to deep holes
Back-bouncing has become the preferred method for many seeking the mighty chinook. This method works well for all species as you'll be using good roe for bait. The idea is to position

the boat just above the hole and bounce your presentation into the hole and hold it there. You'll want enough lead to hit the bottom and hold, but as you lift up on your weight, the current will bounce it down a little further each time. By doing this, the angler has control over where the presentation is. Once the bait is positioned in the hole you won't want it to become stagnant. Keep lifting the presentation gently off the bottom and letting it back down. As long as you don't feed it any more line it will settle back down in the hole.

The bite is very subtle. You'll feel a slight tick most times and know it's not the bottom; get ready but do not set the hook until the fish commits. This can be the hardest part of back-bouncing as the anticipation with the rod in your hand can become overpowering, but too quick of a hook-set will result in a missed fish. Since your bait is not drifting downstream they're in no hurry to swipe it; let them suck on it for a while and when they commit, stick it to them.

Species Specific

Chinook
Slow, deep holes work best for this method. Well-milking eggs along with shrimp are extremely effective. The use of just eggs or sandshrimp alone will also work if the combo doesn't. Don't be afraid of putting a big cluster on, you want the fish to stick around and munch on it.

Back bouncing for chinook.

Divers						
Species	Rod	Rating	Action	Reel	Line	Leader
Steelhead	7'6" to 8'6"	8 - 15lbs	Extra Fast	200 Baitcaster	Braid: 30 - 50lb	Mono: 12-15lb
Coho	7'6" to 8'6"	8 - 15lbs	Extra Fast	200 to 300 Baitcaster	Braid: 20 - 50lb	Mono: 12-15lb
Chinook	7'6" to 8'6"	10 - 20lbs	Extra Fast	300 Baitcaster	Braid: 20 - 65lb	Mono: 20-25lb
Chum	7'6" to 8'6"	10 - 17lbs	Extra Fast	200 to 300 Baitcaster	Braid: 20 - 50lb	Mono: 15-20lb

A batch of fresh coho salmon.

Plunking

Lure: Bait, Plugs

Water: Slow to moderate, mid to deep holes

Plunking is another traditional steelheading method, and it was made for fresh bait. The idea behind plunking is to hold the presentation on the bottom with a heavy sinker, waiting for the fish to come to the presentation rather than going to the fish as the drift-angler does. Well-milking eggs create a scent trail in the water, helping draw fish to the bait. A winged bobber adds to the attraction and will keep attracting even after the bait has all but disappeared from the egg loop.

Big, deep, slow-moving slots are most effective for plunking. Reading water is very important here as the hole must be the path of least resistance so the majority of the fish will choose to travel through your slot.

It's important to check your bait at least every 15 minutes as the current will continue to eat away at it. Change your bait every time you reel in to ensure it's fresh and milking.

Using plugs has also come into the equation when plunking and is a good alternative when bait is prohibited. If bait is allowed, use it.

Species Specific

Steelhead

Well-milking eggs, combined with a Spin-N-Glo, is a great method for steelhead under high water conditions.

Back Bouncing

Species	Rod	Rating	Action	Reel	Line	Leader
Coho	8'6" to 10'	8 - 15lbs	Moderate Fast	200 to 300 Baitcaster	Braid: 20 - 50lb or Mono: 15lb	Mono: 12-15lb
Chinook	8'6" to 10'	10 - 20lbs	Moderate Fast	200 to 300 Baitcaster	Braid: 30 - 65lbs or Mono: 20 - 25lb	Mono: 20-25lb
Chum	8'6" to 10'	10 - 17lbs	Moderate Fast	200 to 300 Baitcaster	Braid: 20 - 30lb or Mono: 15 to 20lb	Mono: 15-20lb

Plunking

Species	Rod	Rating	Action	Reel	Line	Leader
Steelhead	8'6" to 10'	8 - 17lbs	Moderate	3500 Spin or 200 - 300 Baitcaster	Braid: 20 - 30lb or Mono: 15lb	Mono: 15lb
Coho	8'6" to 10'	10 - 20lbs	Moderate	3500 Spin or 200 - 300 Baitcaster	Braid: 20 - 30lb or Mono: 15lb	Mono: 15lb
Chinook	8'6" to 10'	10 - 20lbs	Moderate	3500 Spin or 200 - 300 Baitcaster	Braid: 30 - 65lb or Mono: 20 - 25lb	Mono: 20-25lb
Chum	8'6" to 10'	10 - 20lbs	Moderate	3500 Spin or 200 - 300 Baitcaster	Braid: 20 - 30lb or Mono: 15 to 20lb	Mono: 15-20lb

Winged bobbers can be very successful.

Chinook

While plunking and targeting chinook, a good plug can produce fish if eggs are not available or if there is a bait restriction. You can fasten the plug to a snap swivel. Make your cast without the plug attached and let the sinker settle in, then attach the snap swivel with the plug to the main line and allow it to slide down into the river current. It will work its way to the swivel above the weight, so in this case make your dropper about 3 feet long. Do not use a deep-diving plug in this instance as your plug will already be drawn down by the current and will slide down the main line to the swivel. Many times you'll get hit while the plug is working its way down the line.

Trophy-Fish Tactics

Although any salmon or steelhead should be considered a trophy, there are some fish that are in a class above the others and are truly something to marvel at. Steelhead or coho of 20 pounds or more, or a chinook over 50 pounds, are rare specimens that set the bar for anglers.

Steelhead

When focusing on wild native steelhead you need to cover lots of water, from as high in the systems as you can fish all the way down to the mouth. Since these wild fish are not honed-in to the hatchery they will spread throughout the entire system. When rivers are high and colored-up, concentrate your efforts higher in the system and near where clear water enters the system if possible. When the rivers are low and clear concentrate your efforts lower in the system. During native steelhead season don't be afraid to fish bigger baits and lures for the trophy-sized fish.

In areas where bait is not prohibited, drift fishing 6-inch worms has become increasingly popular. The addition of a drift bobber or winged bobber adds to the attraction in good to off-colored water. Just make sure you use a contrasting color for your bobber. Remember, if there's a bait restriction this means no scent either.

Bait: When fishing bait, I like to use a single hook for these bigger fish: A 1/0 for clear water, 2/0 for normal and 3/0 for high and dirty. A larger egg cluster, sandshrimp (whole or tail), prawn tail or squid all work well, just make sure to add some yarn because you want every advantage when trying to keep the hook in the fish's mouth prior to setting it.

Jigs: A jig under a float is my favorite method of fishing, and that goes for trophy steelhead as well. The only difference is I'll take more chances on where I throw my gear. I like to throw in the ugly stuff where I know a big ol' metal head will be lurking. Do I lose a lot of gear? Yes. Do I catch a lot of fish this way? Yes!

The addition of a 3- to 4-inch pink worm tail for these bigger fish has improved my success for native fish considerably.

Paul Ishii about to release a chinook.

The author with a 14-pound plug-caught hen.

They love those pink worms and I love to float-fish. A perfect combination.

In low-visibility situations—weather or water—glow or UV lures have added another level of confidence that your lure will be seen. Hawken Industries even has a Firefly Jig that involves the use of a light stick attached to the jig body. Over the last few years sales of these jigs has been on fire during no-light to low-light conditions.

Spoons and Plugs: Fishing spoons and plugs always seem to get their fair share of bigger fish as well. As previously discussed, they don't provide the numbers but they do provide the trophies. If you're trophy hunting don't be afraid to fish one of these techniques.

Coho

Using the same techniques as described above, a trophy coho is more apt to strike later in the season. Big fish usually trail behind and are pretty much lock-jawed, but a well-presented twitched jig, hootchie jig, or a good hunk of metal, will often result in a "slab" on the end of your line.

Chinook

One of my fondest memories of fishing with my Dad was on the Kenai River in 2000. During that trip four of us managed our limits each of the two days we were there. We caught chinook of 35, 35, 40, 45, 45, 50, 55 and my Dad's true trophy, a 70-pound monster. The big fish took an hour and 10 minutes to bring to the boat and I have it all on video. Dad passed away in 2001.

The first thing you need to do when fishing for trophy chinook is fish a river system that is known for big fish. One of my favorite rivers, the Nushagak, produces more numbers of chinook than any other river I'm aware of, but chances of getting a trophy are minimal. Between my fishing partners and me, we've hooked several hundred chinook over the past few years and our largest to the boat was approximately 35 pounds and was released. A beautiful fish by anyone's standards, but not a trophy. Most trophy chinook are those over 50 pounds.

Big, big baits are the answer for these big brutes. Huge egg clusters with giant Spin-N-Glos are your best choice, followed closely by huge plugs wrapped with sardine. Rivers such as the Kenai River in Alaska or Chetco River in Oregon are beast-producing machines. The Skeena system, along with many rivers along the Washington and Oregon Coast, also produce mammoth salmon each year. Paying attention to catch record reports, which are available to the public, will help you keep track of those that consistently produce big fish.

Chapter 7
ADAPTING TECHNIQUES TO THE GREAT LAKES

Great Lakes chinook.

The origin of salmon and steelhead in the Great Lakes can be traced back to the Pacific Northwest. Years ago stocks of these fish were introduced to the Great Lakes region for several reasons, chief among them being the need for a predatory fish to help control the population of less desirable or "invader" species such as alewives and Asian carp fry. Another reason was to provide more opportunity for the growing sport-angler population. So being of Pacific Northwest heritage, it's no stretch to believe the techniques we use on the West Coast would work on salmon and steelhead in the Great Lakes region.

Since there are no native chinook, coho or steelhead to this region, catch and release is highly encouraged to allow the population of all species to thrive. Both species have existed in the Great Lakes for numerous years now and have adapted to the characteristics of the streams and tributaries that surround this region. So while things may look different from the outside, they all have the same instincts inside. These aren't necessarily the smartest fish with the wild instincts of natives, but they are beautiful and given

the equipment that must be utilized in this region, the fight is more than sufficient to get an adrenaline rush.

The only native species of salmon in the Great Lakes region is the Atlantic salmon. Although stocks have dwindled almost to the point of decimation, efforts have recently been taken to rebuild the stocks of these fish. The same fishing methods used for chinook or coho will also draw strikes from Atlantics, but most anglers do not target them specifically since they still have not rebuilt to the point that they would draw much interest over the other species available.

Pink salmon somehow found their way to the Great Lakes back in the 1950s. Just like on the West Coast, these crazy salmonids tend to wander and establish themselves in bodies of water for which they weren't actually intended. Although Hudson Bay was the original destination for pinks raised in Canada, they found themselves in Lake Superior and Lake Huron. Now Lake Huron has a thriving population of pink salmon, with the majority returning to spawn in the tributaries during odd years. The largest populations of pinks are in Carp River and St. Marys River.

Ready to release.

Although most pinks are caught incidentally while fishing for other species, the locals who target pinks tend to use fly-fishing gear, small spoons, or spinners. Those who really want to have a blast and catch a bunch of these feisty fish should change tactics and follow the lead of those in the Pacific Northwest—think pink! Twitchin' pink jigs will drive these fish nuts and you'll have everyone wondering why you're so successful. If you don't feel like twitchin', put a piece of pink-cured prawn under a float. These are techniques that have never been seen in the Great Lakes...yet!

Most of what makes the two fisheries different in style is the anglers themselves. Taking on the traditional fishing methods of the Europeans and Canadians, fly-fishing and center-pin fishing are pretty much the norm. Rods under 10 feet are rarely seen on the shores. Spinning reels are becoming more and more common, but with noodle rods of 11 feet or more. The Great Lakes is where light-line specialists rule! Super light line—4- to 6-pound for steelhead and coho and 10- to 12-pound line for chinook—are most often used.

The streams can be flooded with anglers as their numbers continue to boom. Unfortunately, loogans (known as "snaggers" to the rest of the world) are more and more prevalent. Those anglers looking for sport have a vast array of opportunities awaiting them.

The majority of the streams and rivers are small in comparison to those in the Pacific Northwest. In fact, you can wade across most of them and casting to the other side is never a problem. Although a few rivers are large enough for a drift boat or sled,

most boat anglers fish the lakes, many times concentrating on the mouths of the streams.

So, how do we adapt the techniques described in this book to the Great Lakes? Pretty simple, just think a little smaller and lighter.

Although there is fishing pretty much year around in the Great Lakes, there are three times of the year when different fishing techniques should be employed for steelhead. During fall, in the middle of the salmon run, is when you can hook the healthiest and best fighting steelhead of the year. Compare these to spring- or summer-run fish on the West Coast.

The fall run is probably the closest of the species that you could compare to a wild fish as they are spookier than their later arriving cousins and, once hooked, have a nasty attitude. They are often overlooked because salmon that are running at the same time are much easier prey. In mid September these fall fish begin to congregate in front of the river mouths. Rains drive a few upstream but the first great push takes place during the first real temperature drop. The dropping temperature will start their spawning instincts and then it's game on. Small jigs or eggs, from a single to a roe sack of 2 or 3 eggs, with the smallest float you can utilize are key for finding these wary fish.

The waters of the Great Lakes tend to be much colder than those on the West Coast. As the weather becomes even colder and winter hits, ice starts to form around the edges of the lakes and on the shores of the rivers and streams. As the water temperature drops

River mouths are popular fishing areas in the Great Lakes.

it becomes even more important to be stealthy and present much slower presentations with less flash and a more natural look. A float and jig under almost still conditions is an effective way to draw a strike from steelhead, even when ice is forming on the stream.

Nymphing is a very effective technique for Great Lakes steelhead in low clear water. Success rates are very high for those that master this technique, but by applying techniques from the Pacific Northwest we can do even better. A 1/32-ounce jig (or 1/64) in natural colors fished under a float is the perfect combination for drawing strikes from finicky steelhead. And that's not a typo— as small as 1/64 ounce to imitate a nymph! This technique is best used with a center-pin rod and reel since the presentation is so light that any other rod/reel combination may not be able to drop it in lightly enough above the hole so as to not spook the fish.

Don't rule out the standard colors of the Pacific Northwest when float-fishing. Pinks, peaches and whites will produce in most any water. Remember, these fish came from the Pacific Northwest so they still have those same natural instincts in their genetics. It's pretty difficult to make a double-beaded marabou jig in 1/64 once, but the marabou minus the beads works exceptionally well in the low clear waters of Great Lakes streams. When the water darkens up, those natural colored jigs can't be seen, so bring out the brighter fluorescent colors.

In the springtime, as the temperatures begin to rise and the water starts to warm up as well, steelhead start their journey back down to the lakes. They have already spawned and are now looking for food. They are aggressive biters at this time but they're also "downriver" fish having already fulfilled their spawning duties. I encourage fishermen to leave these fish alone. They are tired and beat up and need to return to the lake so that hopefully they'll become healthy enough to make the trip again.

The waters of this region tend to blow out quickly because of the low flows. Not good news when you're fishing, but great news for the upcoming inflow of salmon or steelhead about to move upstream with the oncoming of rain and higher water flows. For both salmon and steelhead the best time to hit these streams is when the water starts to drop and clear up after a rain. It won't take long for them to get back to crystal clear, so while it's "steelhead green" hit it!

When it comes to drift fishing, again light setups are the key. Single or double split shots are about it for weight, and instead of clusters of roe use a roe sack with only 2 to 3 eggs in the mesh as this is most effective. Sometimes only a single egg is required. Because of the light presentation a center-pin rod will also work in this case, but noodle rods seem to rule the rivers for drifting.

Mesh now comes in several colors and sometimes they're just different enough from everything else that's been floating by that it will trigger a strike. Chartreuse mesh with some bright red eggs has been a steady producer for those who have used this combination. The addition of a small tuft of yarn works great for added attraction, scent disbursement and sticking in the fish's mouth. You do not want the yarn to extend beyond the bend of the hook.

The mighty Niagara River.

Mark Par does battle in a small Great Lakes stream.

When seeking coho and chinook early in the season (early fall) spoons are the go-to method. As the fish are milling around the river mouths waiting for a push of rain to draw them up the river, small spoons like a Little Cleo or BC Steel can start a hot bite. Bait always works, and for those who prefer float-fishing spawn sacks with 3 to 5 eggs are key and should be fished with the lightest rig you can get away with. Spinning reels are quite prevalent because of the light presentations. When the water clouds up, bump up the number of eggs in your roe sack as well. It's not uncommon to fish a mesh sack with up to a dozen eggs under higher, darker water conditions.

As the season progresses and the salmon begin to make their journey up the rivers and streams, they become lock-jawed, even more so than in the Pacific Northwest. In this case you'll need to fish something that will intimidate them and cause them to strike out of aggression rather than hunger. A fairly common tactic in the Great Lakes region is drifting large Egg Sucking Leeches or Woolly Buggers.

On those rivers large enough for a drift boat or sled, pulling plugs is a popular method. Pretty much the same technique as on the West Coast except you'll want to back them down much more slowly. Creating a "wall of death" with each plug equidistant from the boat is key. These fish don't seem to be as aggressive as in the Pacific Northwest, so we have to think about backing them down into a tight spot where they'll attack out of fear.

For salmon, all the techniques discussed previously in Chapter 6 will work; but slow down, lighten up and reduce the size. These fish are not very aggressive and sometimes must be coaxed into biting. A small bait or lure presented slowly will typically result in more strikes.

Chapter 8
CARING FOR YOUR CATCH

A trio ready for the trip home.

Whether or not you plan to catch and keep, or catch and release, please respect the fish. They are beautiful creatures and we need them to be around for future generations to enjoy as well.

It's funny how many puzzled looks I see on people's faces when after a successful fishing trip they ask how much fish I brought home and most times my answer is "none". I'm not saying I don't eat fish, I love it, but my wife and I can only eat so much. I also supply my Mom with fish throughout the year, plus my neighbors and some co-workers too. But I can only keep so much and I actually get more satisfaction out of releasing a fish than I do by bonking it on the head. Hatchery fish are raised with the intent to be harvested. Many will argue that you should bonk all hatchery fish so they don't interfere with and contaminate the gene pool of native fish. I'll tell you, if I'm having a great day and know there are plenty of fish around, I'll release several hatchery fish just so I can

keep fishing. There are also times when I'll keep native salmon. If the Game Department is allowing native salmon retention on the river, then they should have enough in the hatchery for escapement to keep producing. However, when it comes to a native steelhead—absolutely, positively, without a doubt do not kill it.

The first part of releasing a fish is catching one. By reading this book, you are gaining knowledge that will lead you to be more successful. If you are planning on releasing fish, how you play them can help result in a healthy fish being released. It may sound strange, but you'll actually want to play the fish more aggressively than you normally would. If you break one off, hey, you were going to release the fish anyway, right? But there are reasons behind the more aggressive approach, mostly so a fish does not become over-exerted and lack the stamina to sustain itself after being released. This doesn't mean we need to use meat rods and horse the fish in; just a little extra tension on the drag system will do it.

Next we want to make sure not to beach a fish that we are going to release. Sand and mud are brutal on a fish and bringing them to the shore will only increase the amount of foreign substances entering the fish through its gills. A nice low spot in the river that is filled with rocks works best. If fishing from a boat, bring the fish to the side and tail it. Bringing it in the boat or netting the fish will only decrease its survival rate and may be illegal depending on where you're fishing. Remove the hook, trying not to make the insertion point any wider. If the hook has been swallowed, cut the leader.

Pictures are great and we all love to see them. Keep the fish in the water while the photographer is getting ready. Once ready, gently lift the fish into position by holding the tail section behind the adipose fin with the other hand cradling underneath near the pectoral fins. Water dripping from the fish will also add a fresh effect showing that the fish was just taken from the water. If you're not allowed to remove the fish from the water, don't. You can still take awesome pictures with a part of the fish remaining in the water, as is required in Washington State. A polarizing filter on your camera's lens can improve your pictures by cutting some of the reflections and glare on the water.

Before actually releasing the fish make sure it's ready to go on its own. By facing upriver and allowing the water to flow through the fish's gills, it will gain strength back and replenish the oxygen it spent while you were playing it. You'll know when the fish is ready. A successful release oftentimes ends with a splash to your face… Think of it as a high-five for a job well done.

For those fish you're going to keep, make sure and give it a solid thump between the eyes or on the snout. For high-quality food fare the most important step is to bleed the fish out. With a sharp knife, cut both sides of the gills. This will not only make for better table fare, but it will also get rid of the blood in the roe which makes for better bait.

I like to put the fish in a fish box or cooler with ice. It's important to keep the fish as cold as possible.

Don't drag your fish on the side of your boat with a rope, or tie them up and let them die slowly on the side of the river. Not only is this inhumane, but it will also increase the lactic acid level and give the fish a different flavor that, in my opinion, is not favorable.

Clean the fish as soon as your fishing day has come to an end, or if you're taking a break from the action.

Most people prefer to fillet their fish but there are still fans of the good old-fashioned fish steak.

A sharp fillet knife is a must. Not only will it make your job easier, it's also safer. A fillet glove is also a great option for those of us that tend to nick ourselves.

A properly filleted salmon not only tastes good but looks good too.

How to Fillet

Cut all the way through the belly section to remove the insides. Make the next cut straight down next to the gill plate, perpendicular to the backbone, and stop cutting once you've reached the backbone (don't cut through it). While holding the knife against the backbone, turn it 90° so the cutting edge faces the tail and the blade is parallel to the backbone. Then, while holding the belly flap up with one hand, start cutting towards the tail, with the blade parallel to the backbone, or angled just slightly towards the backbone, so it rides against it. Use the backbone as your guide. At first, you'll be cutting through the rib bones, so the first part might take a little effort, this is why you want a sharp knife! Continue to hold the belly meat up so the blade doesn't get accidently cut it. Work the blade along the backbone, back towards the tail. You'll want the blade to pass just above the dorsal fin, leaving the most meat possible on your fillet. Keeping the blade against the backbone, pass just above the adipose fin as well. At the tail of the fish, run your blade out along the backbone, and then angle it slightly upward, through the skin.

Once you've got your first fillet cut, set it aside and flip your fish over. Again, cut down just behind the gill plate, perpendicular to the backbone, through the entire fillet, but not through the backbone. Hold the belly meat up and start cutting through the rib bones, moving the blade towards the tail in the same motion you did on the first side.

Place the fillets with the bellies facing away from you in order to remove the first one or two ribs from the front of the fillet.

These ribs are positioned slightly differently from the rest of the ribs and if you don't remove them first, they cause problems in this next step. Starting near where the backbone used to be, cut just under the ribs. To do this easily takes a delicate touch. You want to angle the knife so it's angled slightly upward towards the ribs, maximizing the amount of meat you leave on the fillet. You also want to put a little pressure down on the knife lengthwise, giving it a slight bend, so it follows the ribs more closely. This is where a true fillet knife comes in handy, because true fillet knives have the proper blade thickness that allows you to bend the blade with just the right pressure. Continue to cut and lift the ribs out.

Now that the ribs are removed, we need to do a little delicate "finish" work to make the fillets look presentable. Much of this is a matter of personal preference, some people don't do much trimming at all, others go hog-wild, so feel free to improvise and do what you think is practical. The first thing to do is remove the fins and the cartilage around them. Removing the belly meat on the fillet is optional and personal preference.

Removing pin bones is a pain in the butt, but to have a boneless piece of meat it's a necessary evil. The first thing you want to do is to hold the fillet from underneath, so the pin bones poke out a bit more and are easier to get at. A pair of needle-nose pliers works well, but a pair of forceps or hemostats are even better.

Steaks

Cutting steaks is pretty simple. Assuming the fish has already been cleaned, place a sharp knife just behind the gill plate like

Chinook salmon.

you would to fillet the fish. As you cut straight down, continue cutting through the backbone and through the whole fish. I don't like to use a fillet knife in this case because it will dull it up pretty quickly. A traditional chef's knife works much better here. Move the knife over for the desired thickness and continue until the fish is all cut up. Trim the belly fat off of each steak for a nicer appearance.

Smoking Fish

It seems like everyone loves smoked fish! In my opinion, salmon are the best fish you can smoke. Steelhead smokes up well too, but doesn't quite have the flavor I'm looking for.

There are many different smokers out there and a ton of smoking recipes. I think one of the main variables that will help in producing award-winning smoked salmon or steelhead is the smoker temperature. I smoke all my fish at a consistent 160 degrees.

Cutting your fish into portion-sized pieces not only allows the brine to penetrate the fish better prior to smoking, but also makes it much more convenient for storage. Smoked fish, when stored in vacuum packs, will easily last a year in the freezer.

Recipes

A nicely smoked filet looks gorgeous. For special occasions, watch and see if this isn't the biggest hit on the table!

Smoked Salmon

This is by far the best smoked salmon recipe I've ever used. It was developed by my friend Ron Harrington. Feel free to experiment with changing the quantities of the ingredients a little, such as adding more pepper or garlic, but the recipe as written is superb.

Smoked Candy
• 1 cup white sugar
• 1 cup brown sugar
• 1/3 cup salt
• 2 Tbsp garlic powder
• 2 Tbsp onion powder
• 2 Tbsp pepper

Cut fish into pieces no larger than 6"x 4".

Mix all ingredients in a bowl. Place fish into mix, coating all of it. Place fish skin side down in a second glass bowl (the bigger the better). Layer the fish until done. The fish will start to emulsify so don't fill to the top.

Cover with plastic wrap and put in the fridge for 2 days, rotating fish from top to bottom after 1 day. After 2 days rinse the fish slightly, gently shake off water and put on smoker rack. Let sit for thirty minutes. Preheat smoker then place fish in it for six to eight hours depending on thickness using alder, hickory or your preferred smoking wood. Fish should look caramel in color when done.

For a sweeter taste: brush on honey or pure maple syrup during the last hour of smoking.

Nushagak Candied Salmon

This is a favorite of mine courtesy of my wife, Theresa. Recipe is for 1" thick salmon; vary cooking time depending on thickness or desired texture

Can't you just taste it.

• Salmon
• Salt
• Pepper
• Garlic Salt
• Lemon
• Brown Sugar
• Butter

Pre-heat oven to 350 degrees. Place salmon fillet in baking dish. Salt, pepper and garlic salt to taste. Squeeze juice from whole lemon over fish. Cover dish with foil and place in pre-heated oven. Bake for 20 minutes. Remove from oven and pat a thin layer of brown sugar over entire fillet. Melt enough butter to drizzle over fillet (approx. 1 tablespoon per pound of salmon). Place uncovered in oven for additional 10-15 minutes until fish begins to flake apart.

Theresa's Salmon Cakes

Oh my, if you like salmon you will love these. My wife developed this recipe using ingredients I like. This is a favorite of the neighbors, co-workers and ours.
• 2 pounds boneless, cooked salmon
• 1/2 lemon (squeezed over salmon)
• 1 Tbsp dill
• 1/4 tsp salt
• 1 tsp pepper
• 1/2 onion (chopped)
• 3 cloves garlic (chopped)

Bake in pre-heated 350-degree oven until salmon flakes apart. Approximately 20 to 25 minutes for 1-inch-thick fillet.
• 1 Large egg
• 2 Tbsp milk
• 6 Green onions
• 1 cup Italian bread crumbs
• 1/4 tsp salt

Beat egg and milk together. Stir in remaining ingredients, including cooked salmon. Shape into cakes or patties roughly 3 inches in diameter. Add vegetable oil in a fry pan on medium heat. Fry until golden brown on both sides.

Enjoy!

Chapter 9
WOMEN, SALMON AND STEELHEAD

April Vokey with a slab—absolutely gorgeous.

There are no teams when it comes to salmon and steelhead fishing, just buddies out for a good time. And for those of you that are really hooked, you don't even need a buddy. I've spent countless hours on the rivers enjoying the heck out of a river all by myself, and in fact sometimes prefer it that way. The solitude and being one-on-one with nature is a feeling that can't be explained or understood without first-hand experience.

For some reason when it comes to fishing, most see it as a man's sport. How often do you see an article or book where anglers are referred to as fisherwomen? Not often. But women can be a part of the sport and be very successful. Many times I've been fishing with a female angler that out-fishes everyone, sound familiar? Women have to work harder to be accepted as anglers so they pay more attention to detail and follow through with those techniques better than us men.

I've been fortunate to fish with many different people of all skill levels. When a woman is serious about fishing and puts the time in, there's no reason she won't be as successful as a man under the same conditions. The perception always seems to be that a woman on the river is a rarity and she can't hack it. Truth be known, given the chance women can make some of the best fishing partners you can have.

I wish I could put myself in a woman's shoes to convey what it's like as a woman playing in what's perceived as a man's sport,

but I wouldn't be able to do it justice. Below are two women's views on what it takes to be a successful female angler. Put aside their good looks and view them as anglers. They have much to offer the salmon and steelhead world and my hope is that by reading their stories we can get even more women involved.

"I have a confession to make. I've always been a sucker for a woman casting a fly rod. I can't help but watch in awe as she casts effortlessly into the cool breeze, gently throwing mends upriver, concentrating on her fly's presentation before stripping the line back in and preparing to cast again. I try so hard not to stare but, the truth is I just can't help myself.

Don't get me wrong, I love to watch a tight loop cast from just about any angler, man or woman, but there's just something different about a cast kissed with a feminine touch."

This beautiful statement was penned by Ms. April Vokey.

April Vokey is a full-time guide, instructor and columnist. She can be found at www.flygal.ca. Best known for her steelhead work with a fly, April has caught numerous trophy steelhead and her picture has adorned many covers of magazines. April is considered a fly-fishing expert and primarily targets steelhead during both the summer and winter months on renowned rivers such as the Dean and other productive streams.

"Getting started was intimidating" explains April, "I had a lot of questions and with no one to answer them, I made my way to

Bryanna Zimmerman is all smiles while releasing this beautiful fish.

the library and took out every book I could find on different species of fish and methods of catching them."

With books only came part of the answers, but she yearned for more.

"For this, I had to seek help from somebody with experience, so I headed to my local tackle shop. Little do they know it, but that was a day I will never forget. Barriers dropped, and fears were forgotten, as I was welcomed with friendly faces, sincerely interested in showing me how to grow in the sport. In return, that shop gained a loyal customer, never too proud to ask for advice and always eager to share my reports and experiences. It is a relationship I strongly urge any aspiring angler to commit to.

"As a firm believer in equal opportunity and a fishing buddy to both men and women, I have spent countless days on the water with a wide ranging assortment of anglers. Over the years, some days have proven to be undeniably frustrating, and others unbelievably picture-perfect. I'm simply a woman who likes to play in the water, rather than a diva or a feminist—a serious angler in touch with my feminine side, who spends all of my free time chasing fish in the hope that they, in turn, will chase my fly. You can be certain that there are more of us out there than you might think there are and, with time, as each woman begins to break through the subtle barrier of what has been up until now a 'boys only club', we are slowly finding each other and establishing our own niche."

Bryanna Zimmerman is an up and comer in the salmon and steelhead world and is turning heads on rivers throughout the Pacific Northwest. Bryanna is the "Steelhead U Girl" and blogs her updates and adventures on the Steelhead University site. She also started a new website for women anglers, www.steelheadgirls.com. Bryanna is a strong supporter of women anglers and an advocate for more women's fishing gear and apparel.

Here is Bryanna's story:

The initial reaction of a man after hearing that I fish is, "No... You? Really?" followed by, "Wow, that's awesome!" The initial reaction of a man after seeing me on the river is one of two things: eyes rolling followed by small scoff or an invite to share the hole; usually the latter. There are plenty of high-fives, "good jobs," and "way to go's" once the fish are caught, and almost always new friends everywhere I go.

Being a woman and being taught how to fish is hard! Both the teacher and student must have immense amounts of patience. There is so much discouragement at first and so many feelings of defeat and wanting to give up. If someone told me that I would have a burning feeling inside of me to fish, I would have called them crazy. I wanted to fish, but by no means was it a necessity. Once I caught that first fish is when that feeling began, but I just hadn't realized it yet.

My boyfriend taught me slowly, patiently, and praised me for everything I did right no matter how big or small the action was.

Adrienne Comeau about to release a beauty.

Of course there were plenty of tears on the water and plenty days where pouting on the bank was how most of my time was spent, but I couldn't fight that feeling of wanting another fish. The fishing trips needed to stay fun. It wasn't about how many fish we could catch or catching limits, it needed to be about the time spent on the water. Spending quality time with good people. Laughing a lot and accomplishing a lot. To this day, even after the obsession has embedded itself, it's still to simply have a good time. Catching no fish and having an amazing day is better than catching limits but having bad attitudes and confrontations.

It was not enjoyable to be in the rain, sometimes around rude people, a lot of cigarettes, and cold. But there was a burning desire to catch more fish somewhere inside of me. I yearned for the feeling of having something tug the end of my line. I soon realized that it wasn't the sport of the fishing that was difficult to enjoy or to grasp—I truly enjoyed myself when I was on the water and I just couldn't say no to a trip and found myself actually mentioning that I wanted to go again—it was the leaky waders, the waterproof jackets that seemed to absorb every rain drop. It was the reels that were too heavy for my wrist and the tackle bags that were too big for my shoulder. It was not having friends that fished with me. No girls to gossip with on river that matched the companionship I had at cheer practice; and when I did tell my friends, they thought I was crazy. My family didn't understand why I missed barbecues and spent the little free time that I had on the river.

It was once I realized that salmon and steelhead had stolen a piece of my heart that I chose to really begin investing in the necessary items that would alleviate any discomfort that I had. The hardest part about this was finding quality, solid women's attire. If staying dry in the Northwest was mostly what was making it uncomfortable, I needed waders and jackets that would last and wouldn't leave me with wet socks and sleeves. That was the first step. The second was to test and figure out what rods and reels did what and testing and playing around to find what was comfortable and fit me. Things in the fishing world are not made for women. They aren't made to accommodate the things that women think

about that perhaps men don't. Once I could find what made it comfortable, the rest fell into place.

My girlfriends realized that my pompoms were retired and began to be interested in my excursions! They asked about it, they loved my pictures, they loved my stories and they no longer thought I was crazy. My family wanted to go, I met other fishermen's girlfriends who wanted to fish as well, and I figured out how to hang with the guys, just being one of the guys.

My parents soon realized this was my passion and it wasn't just a fad. They had a very hard time understanding because they couldn't enjoy it with me or watch me enjoy it like they did when they would come to my football games or performances. I couldn't just haul them along without them having waders and extra rods and tackle, so it took a while before they began to understand. Now they are my biggest fans. They are so proud and so intrigued (plus they get free salmon whenever they want).

The men are beyond supportive. Of course I get the occasional weary look, but being polite and friendly goes a long way. I realized that most fishermen are not rude, they do not have bad attitudes and actually enjoy conversation. I almost always have a spot on the river to fish and always have free advice and tips. When I catch a fish, there are far more "woo hoo's" and "right on's" than when another man catches a fish. It's incredibly encouraging and makes the experience more enjoyable.

It is different to be a women fishing than it is for a man and it's honestly a strange concept that you have to grasp once you realize that you truly *need* to be on the water. You long for the outdoors. You dream of seeing scales and bobber downs. It's a whole other world and it just took over my life. It's probably the best thing that has ever happened to me. Never forgetting what it felt like to catch my first steelhead by myself. The satisfaction and feeling of accomplishment took over my body for weeks. The feeling of achieving goals in fishing extended to my everyday life and I made new goals and ambitions in my personal life. I not only learned how to accept defeat by losing fish or not catching any, but I learned how to use that feeling of defeat and turn it into motivation and stronger desires.

Conclusion

NICK PUJIC

April Vokey has one of the most beautiful casts you'll ever see.

Salmon and steelhead success are now within your grasp. By reading the material in this book you have all the knowledge you need to get on the road to being a successful salmon and steelhead angler. By putting this knowledge to use you will increase your odds substantially. A day on the water is better than a day at work, but a successful day is what we're after.

Success comes in many forms. But, most of all, enjoyment of the outdoors and the passion for salmon and steelhead fishing are the reasoning behind publishing this book. I have been blessed by being able to learn from some of the best-known Pacific Northwest anglers and from my own experiences on the water. Whether you're a beginning angler just hoping to enter this wonderful world of fishing or already an accomplished angler, following the guidelines I have outlined will get you to the next level. I continue to learn all the time and am thankful for each day on the water. I cherish all that I have learned to maximize my effectiveness on the water. I hope you take my advice and do the same.

The more you fish, the more often you will come back to this book for reference. The more knowledge retained will result in more fish.

Above all, have fun… Peace.

Appendix A

Resources

Steelhead University
Salmon & steelhead fishing education. Articles, resources, reviews and reports for salmon and steelhead. Washington, Oregon, Idaho and Alaska. www.steelheaduniversity.com

Regulations, Seasons, Fish Counts, Catch Records, Run Predications, Smolt Releases, Conservation and the latest fishing news:

• Washington Department of Fish & Wildlife: http://wdfw.wa.gov/fishing/

• Oregon Department of Fish & Wildlife: http://www.dfw.state.or.us/resources/fishing/

• Idaho Department of Fish and Game: http://fishandgame.idaho.gov/public/fish/

• California Department of Fish & Game: http://www.dfg.ca.gov/fish/Fishing/

• U.S. Geological Survey: Water data information for all 50 United States. Provides stream-flow information, including Cubic Feet Per Second (CFS) and River Height. http://waterdata.usgs.gov/nwis

• National Oceanic and Atmospheric Associations (NOAA) - Northwest River Forecast Center. Provides river and weather forecasts, river height, temperature and flow for Washington, Oregon, Idaho and California.

• NOAA Northwest: http://www.nwrfc.noaa.gov/rfc/

• NOAA Alaska: http://aprfc.arh.noaa.gov/

British Columbia
• BC Fisheries and Agriculture: Regulations, seasons, fish counts, catch records, run predications, smolt releases, conservation and the latest fishing news. http://www.agf.gov.bc.ca/fisheries/index.htm

• Province of British Columbia: River and water flow forecasts. http://bcrfc.env.gov.bc.ca/index.htm

Great Lakes
• Great Lakes Information Network: Provides weather and river forecasts for the Great Lakes. http://www.great-lakes.net/envt/water/levels/flows.html

Fishing Knots
Animated Knots by Grog: Provides step-by-step instructions for tying fishing knots, including what knot to use when. http://www.animatedknots.com/indexfishing.php

Appendix B

Bait Cures

Good bait can be priceless to the salmon or steelhead angler; it can be tough to come by as well. While there's nothing better than a perfectly cured batch of eggs, there's nothing worse than rotten or improperly cured eggs. If you don't like the eggs you cured, why would the fish?

"I can't tell you how many pounds of primo eggs I have ruined over the years by trying new things," says guide Phil Stephens, "these days I have narrowed down my process in curing bait and one cure that never lets my clients or me down is an easy recipe I started mixing up a few years ago."

There are many great egg cures commercially available these days and everyone seems to have their favorite. New egg cures on the scene may be good, may be fantastic, try them out if you want to experiment. But if you have a limited egg supply it's always been my recommendation you go with one of the cures that have been around for many years. There's a reason why they stick around, obviously people are buying the product, but to keep buying the product indicates a cure that works.

Know what you'll be fishing for before preparing your cured eggs. Salmon generally prefer a large, soft egg that milks a lot and

Phil Stephens' Simple but Effective Cure

• 1 Container of Beau Macs Pro Glow
• 1/2 cup sugar
• 1 cup borax. I like 20 Mule Team, but whatever you have access to will work.

Combine all three ingredients, make sure it's mixed together well and any clumps of borax are broken up. If there are a few small clumps no worries, but less is best.

Cut eggs into bait-size chunks and place into a container of some type. I like stainless-steel but I often use glass or a large zip-lock bag.

Sprinkle a liberal amount of your newly combined cure onto your eggs...don't worry if you think you added a touch too much, it'll be OK. Make sure all the eggs are coated with cure.

Let stand uncovered in a cool area about an hour then drain off juice while keeping eggs in the container. Don't worry if eggs shrivel up a little, they usually do.

After the first drain off, let stand about 4 hours and drain off again while leaving eggs in container for a few more hours. If flies or bugs are a problem, put a piece of cheesecloth over the eggs while they drain.

If the eggs are hard little BB's, I place them in a zip-lock bag and put it in the fridge for a couple days; those little BB's will reabsorb whatever juice there is left on them and turn into perfect bait.

If the eggs are still soft after the second drain then I air-dry them for about 6 hours. After that, place eggs in a zip-lock bag and move to the refrigerator for a couple days before freezing.

Once frozen, vacuum pack them and they will last for years. A tip: When you bring them out of the freezer make sure to puncture the bag so the eggs don't get squished while thawing.

Note: While this is Phil's preferred curing don't be afraid to change it up a little. My suggestion is to substitute Pautzke Borax 'o Fire when setting up eggs for salmon. Pautzke has krill and can trigger a salmon bite when other cures won't.

Quick Shrimp Cure

Here's a quick, easy and very good alternative to eggs and, for me, my number one bait through the summer months for summer steelhead. Winter steelhead, coho, kings as well chums also love this easily available bait.

What you need:
1. Go to your local grocery store's fish department. What you're looking for is shrimp with head off, shell on. Most grocery stores carry them thawed, but if frozen purchase them in one-pound bags. Once you've found them you have to decide what size you need. To me this isn't important because we're cutting them into small chunks anyway. For about $3.99 a pound you have an endless supply of bait, close to home, and you don't even have to worry about making room for all your bait in your own freezer.
2. Grab your favorite bait cure. Pautzke's, Beau Mac, Pro Glo, Pro Cure, Amerman's, Quick Cure, take your pick!
3. A glass or stainless-steel bowl. If you don't have one, don't fret, a gallon-sized zip-lock bag will work wonders in times of need (just make sure you have a high-quality bag or you'll have a mess if it leaks).

Here's all you need to do:

• Place your shrimp, shell on, in the container of your choice.
• Sprinkle a small amount of your favorite egg cure on them.
• Mix well, and let stand for a few hours.
• Strain off all the juice.
• Cut into bait-sized chunks (1/2 inch to 1 inch).

This stuff is a steelhead favorite fished just like roe, yet it's cleaner, stays on the hook longer, is more readily available, and not a pain in the behind to use.

contains chemicals. Yep, they're hooked...chemical junkies. Commercially produced cures have plenty of chemicals so make sure and follow the directions on the package properly to get the eggs milking out.

Steelhead, on the other hand, are a little more finicky and prefer nice, firm, durable eggs that have a slightly sweeter taste and not necessarily all the chemicals.

One thing that cannot be stressed enough is the care and preparation of your bait prior to the curing process. Bleeding fish and keeping roe cold and free of any type of contaminates such as dirt, sand, etc. will make for a better end product. By bleeding the fish this will eliminate blood from the membrane of the egg sack. Get the roe sacks out of the fish and into zip-lock bags as soon as you can.

It's always a good rule to cure bait as soon as possible after getting home from a day of fishing. If, for some reason, you cannot cure roe that day, wait no more than three days before curing. Any longer than that and I wouldn't waste my time or cure because you're probably not going to get the eggs you want.

Swanny's 3-2-1 Nushagak Recipe

Fishing in a river that has 100k-plus returning chinook gives you an opportunity to experiment to find out what works best. It's not is you cure going to work, because it will, it's more how well is it going to work.

Below is a compilation put together by Bill "Swanny" Swan after many years of experimenting to find the right cure on the Nushagak River. This is the same cure used when two buddies and I hooked 175 and 191 chinook in consecutive days.

- 3 cups raw sugar
- 2 cups borax, dehydrate (A mild form of borax that won't dry out your eggs)
- 1 cup sea salt
- 1/2 cup strawberry Jell-O mix (adds color and additional sweetener)
- 1 tablespoon Pautzke Krill Fire Power (crucial to waters with high krill content)

Mix all ingredients thoroughly by pouring them in a gallon zip-lock bag and continuously working the bag until you get the ingredients properly mixed.

Pour contents into a shaker bottle to be used for application. Note: If you are higher up in a river system, add sodium sulfites to your mixture. Salmon expend their sulfite supply the closer they get to their spawning grounds so sulfites are a great attractant above tidal water.

Sprinkle enough of the cure to cover the eggs and let air-dry for 4-6 hours depending on the tackiness and firmness you desire.

Once you're satisfied with the texture, place in zip-lock baggies and put in the refrigerator for a couple days. They'll be fine in the fridge for weeks, but if you aren't planning on using them soon freeze them.

Duane's "Secret" Pautzke Recipes

Duane Inglin is a Pautzke Mixologist! When Pautzke needs new chemicals and ingredients tested they rely on Duane's expertise to make sure only the finest products hit the shelf. Here's a couple of his "secret" recipes he's agreed to share in my book.

Eggs
- Gallon zip-lock bag
- 1/2 bottle of Fire Brine (choose color)
- 1/4 cup BorX O Fire (match color)
- 1/4 cup white sugar

- Can do 4 to 6 egg skeins, depending on their size. Soak up to 4 hours. 2 skeins soak approximately 2 1/2 to 3 hours.
- Mix & match colors of Fire Brine and BorX O Fire to create the color desired.
- Add the extras, like anise oil and Fire Power Krill Powder

Coon Shrimp: (60 to 80 count)
- 1 Qrt. Jar
- 1 full bottle of Nectar (choose color)
- 1/2 bottle of Fire Brine
- 1/4 cup raw sugar, 1/4 cup white sugar
- 1/4 cup Non-Iodized Sea Salt
- 1/2 to 1 Teaspoon Fire Power Krill
- 1/4 cup rock salt
- 1/4 cup BorX O Fire
- 1/2 to 1 Teaspoon Fire Power Krill

Top off with distilled water.
For variations top off with additional Fire Brine or additional Nectar. You can also add sweeteners, anise, or vanilla (6 to 10 drops)

This is a cold brine for coon shrimp that have been cooked or flash boiled. The shrimp are pre-cooked so cold brine works great. Give the shrimp 2 to 3 weeks soak time to acquire full color and allow for the salts and sugars to cure the meat of the shrimp. This makes the shrimp much more durable and they will fish much better. Color choice is up to you. My number one go-to is Red Nectar and the Dark Red BorX O Fire. This makes a very good deep red color on my shrimp.

Index

TERRY WIEST has over 37 years of experience fishing for salmon and steelhead and has the natural ability to teach people how to catch more fish, whether it be in writing, speaking at seminars, or graciously helping others on the water.

Terry is an award-winning author and has published numerous magazine articles, mostly on salmon and steelhead, but also on his many adventures around the Pacific Northwest, Canada, and Alaska doing what he loves to do...fish! He has also contributed to the book, *Pro Tactics for Salmon and Steelhead*. In addition to articles, Terry writes a bi-monthly column, "Westsider" for *Northwest Sportsman Magazine*.

Since 2006, Terry has been the Webmaster and Chief Instructor for Salmon University, the largest salmon fishing website on the West Coast. Terry also hosts and serves as Chief Instructor for Steelhead University, the largest steelhead website on the West Coast. His vast knowledge of fishing and endless dedication is spread throughout both of these fantastic sites.

A familiar face that has graced the cover of many publications, Terry is an icon on the rivers throughout the Pacific Northwest. One of the top, expert jig-fishermen, Terry helped pioneer the method of using a pink worm on a jig head.

You'll also find Terry dedicating his time on the salt fishing for salmon, halibut, and lingcod which he has also published many articles on. In 2007, he won the North Kitsap Puget Sound Anglers Coho Derby and in 2008 he won the coveted Langara Island King Salmon Derby. Terry was welcomed into the Oak Bay Marine Group Captain's Club in 2008 for catching a trophy salmon. He has since repeated this feat for both salmon and halibut.

Terry is an active member of the Northwest Outdoor Writers Association and is Past-President of the South King County Puget Sound Anglers where he is a Lifetime Member. He has spent countless hours sharing his knowledge and experience with others.

Catching hundreds of salmon and steelhead every year, what Terry enjoys most is sharing pictures, stories and memories with all those that will listen in hopes that they too will enjoy his passion as much as he does.

When Does Your Next Adventure Begin?

Thousands of lakes and streams await anglers in Oregon, Washington, Colorado, California and Michigan. Pick almost any spot on the map and chances are there's a fishing spot nearby. Fresh water, salt water; trout, salmon, steelhead, bass, walleye, sturgeon, halibut... the opportunities are endless.

These Maps are a compilations of the all-time most requested fishing map features from *Fishing & Hunting News*—major source of fishing news & information for nearly 50 YEARS! Year after year, the writers, photographers, and map makers of *FHN* went straight to the best local sources for useful, detailed, and in-depth information on top fishing spots. And now you'll find: fish species; seasonal availability; run timing; most productive techniques; best tackle and flies; shore and boat access points; and so much more.

Discover new angling thrills in those places you've heard so much about but have yet to visit! Half the fun is planning and anticipating upcoming fishing trips—whether you're going alone or with friends. All: 8 1/2 x 11 inches, all-color.

COLORADO'S TOP FISHING & HUNTING MAPS
(132 pages, all-color)
SB: $24.95 (COTM)
ISBN-13: 978-1-57188-483-1
UPC: 0-81127-00325-9

MICHIGAN'S TOP FISHING MAPS
(200 pages, all-color)
SB: $29.95 (MITM) Available Spring 2013
ISBN-13: 978-1-57188-496-1
UPC: 0-81127-00342-6

CALIFORNIA'S TOP FISHING MAPS LAKES
(190 pages, all-color)
SB: $24.95 (CTLM) Available January 2013
ISBN-13: 978-1-57188-495-4
UPC: 0-81127-00341-9

OREGON'S TOP FISHING MAPS
(190 pages, all-color)
SB: $24.95 (ORTM)
ISBN-13: 978-1-57188-472-5
UPC: 0-81127-00314-3

WASHINGTON'S TOP FISHING MAPS
(267 pages, all-color)
SB: $29.95 (WATM)
ISBN-13: 978-1-57188-471-8
UPC: 0-81127-00311-2

Lower Deschutes River Fishing and Recreation Map
by John Shewey
Guide to the lower 100 miles of the Deschutes River. 4 3/8 x 11 inches when folded, all color.

$5.95 (LDM)
ISBN-13: 978-1-57188-117-5
UPC: 0-66066-00314-0

1-800-541-9498 www.AmatoBooks.com Fax: 503-653-2766

Lake Maps & Fishing Guides

Throw a dart at a map of Washington and chances are it will land near a good fishing lake. Washington has over 7,000 lakes, 2500+ at alpine levels. You can count on the *Washington Lake Maps & Fishing Guide* to give you everything you need for a successful trip to 40 of Washington's most productive fishing lakes.

As with the popular "*River Maps . . .*" Series, each lake is packed with information, including: Roads and access points; Boat launches; Peak fishing times for various species; Insect hatches and hatch timing; Fly-fishing and conventional tackle techniques; Fishing knots & tackle guide; Important services and accommodations; and so much more. 11 x 15 inches, 48 pages, all-color.

OREGON: SB: $25.00 (ORL)

ISBN-13: 978-1-57188-454-1
UPC: 0-81127-00293-1

WASHINGTON: SB: $25.00 (WAL)

ISBN-13: 978-1-57188-477-0
UPC: 0-81127-00319-8

River Maps & Fishing Guides

Professional guides and expert anglers from each state team up to create these essential guidebooks. These guides feature 25-30 detailed maps covering many miles of river—and that's just the beginning. These maps are packed with information, including: Roads and river access points; Drift-boat and power-boat landings; Peak fishing times for trout, salmon, steelhead, sturgeon, and more; Insect hatches and hatch-timing chart; Fly-fishing and conventional tackle techniques; Fishing knots & tackle guide; Important services & accommodations for anglers, and the list goes on.

Whether you're casting from the bank or fishing from a boat, these guides tell you where to be and when to be there. 11 x 15 inches, 48 pages, all-color.

ALASKA:
SB: $29.95 (AKM)
ISBN-13: 978-1-57188-425-1
UPC: 0-81127-00259-7

CALIFORNIA (NORTHERN):
SB: $29.95 (NCAM)
ISBN-13: 978-1-57188-392-6
UPC: 0-81127-00226-9

IDAHO:
SB: $25.00 (IDM)
ISBN-13: 978-1-57188-455-8
UPC: 0-81127-00294-8

MONTANA:
SB: $25.00 (MTM)
ISBN-13: 978-1-57188-412-1
UPC: 0-81127-00246-7

OREGON:
SB: $25.00 (ORM)
ISBN-13: 978-1-57188-317-9
UPC: 0-81127-00150-7

WASHINGTON:
SB: $25.00 (WAM)
ISBN-13: 978-1-57188-367-4
UPC: 0-81127-00201-6

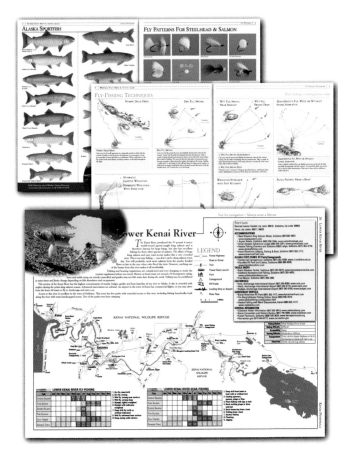

1-800-541-9498 www.AmatoBooks.com Fax: 503-653-2766

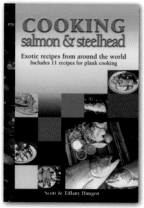
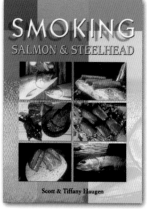

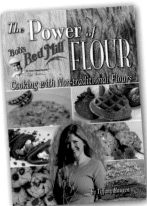